MW01098362

G od
R eadying
A ll
C hristians
E verywhere

Learning to Live for God!

If you have been around Christians (Bible believing and committed) for any length of time, you have heard the public cries of

"GOD, SEND US REVIVAL!"

Sadly, the assumption has always been that when God does finally send this revival, it will come with great signs and wonders! But, is that what the Bible teaches? What if this great revival we have been seeking is already taking place right now all around the world?

It is!

God Readying All Christians Everywhere is a simple, yet powerful tool that will open up your understanding of the Bible in ways you never thought possible. This revival that many have been looking for is not taking place with great "signs and wonders". Instead, it is happening right now in hearts and minds of thousands around the world.

Thanks to courageous pastors, like Pastor Joseph Prince from Singapore and many others, God's GRACE and God's Goodness is bringing revival in the hearts and lives of Believers at unprecedented rates! These miraculous blessings that hundreds of thousands have been experiencing are available to EVERY BELIEVER!

If your heart's desire is to learn to live for God, this book is for you! You may notice that on a few occasions, I will repeat myself or repeat certain verses more than once. This is not an accident. It is being done to help you learn important biblical principles! Learning is a repetitious process. The first time you heard two plus two is four you did not remember it. Most readers of this work will be hearing familiar Bible verses explained in very unfamiliar ways. In learning to live for God, understanding these verses in proper context is key!

In this book, you will examine scriptures that, for many years, you may have thought you knew the meaning. This book will teach you through these scriptures how to understand how God works in the hearts and minds of Believers. It will teach you how God's GRACE, the same GRACE that saved you, is the same GRACE that will keep you and teach you to live for HIM in a right relationship. You will learn how many Bible verses that were meant to set us free have been contorted over the years and have driven many into a life of bondage.

Yes, my friend, Jesus came to set you free! This great revival is taking place right now in preparation for Christ's return. I do not want you to miss out on a single blessing. That's why I wrote this book! Be Blessed.

Pastor Steve

Dedicated to the fine, loving Christians of the
Southern Arizona Community Church,
Green Valley, Arizona

Special Thanks to **Marie Dennis and Nina Keck**
who incalculably improved this writing helping me
to see the forest through the trees! Also my
daughter, **Sarah Riesgo, Riesgo Photography** for
the cover design.

Index

Chapter 1
God's Law is Perfect!

When God gave Moses the Ten Commandments, He set in motion parameters that would change the world with just ten ironclad laws which ideally should be easy to keep.

1. I am the Lord thy God – Thou shall have no other gods before me.
2. Thou shall not have any graven images or likenesses that are in heaven or on the earth.
3. Thou shall not take the name of the Lord in vain.
4. Remember the Sabbath day to keep it holy.
5. Honor your mother and father.
6. Thou shall not kill.
7. Thou shall not commit adultery.
8. Do not steal.
9. Do not lie.
10. Do not covet your neighbor's wife or his goods.

A comprehensive reading of the Ten Commandments can be found in the book of **Exodus Chapter 20.**

Just about every law in society today can trace its roots back to the original Ten Commandments. As of this writing, a statue of Moses holding the Ten Commandments is prominently displayed above the United States Supreme Court Building in Washington, D.C. There are many who would love to see that statue torn down, but that is a subject for an entirely different book.

While God was dealing directly with the children of Israel through Moses, He added another 613 laws requiring that ALL be kept perfectly! To this day, Jewish Rabbis wear a prayer shawl called a Tallit. This white outer garb with blue lines has 613 tassels, or threads on the bottom of it, each representing one of the Mosaic laws.

For whoever shall keep the whole law, and yet stumble in one point, he is guilty of all.
James 2:10

Did you read that? Break one law, and it is as if you have broken all of them! The laws of God are perfect. There is nothing wrong with the laws of God. However, the laws were given to mankind to show just how far short we all are from God's standards and His righteousness. None of us is capable of fulfilling or fully obeying God's laws. NONE of us!

As it is written: "There is none righteous, no, not one."
Romans 3:10

As with the Ten Commandments, the Tabernacle in the Wilderness was also perfect as God laid out His instructions for the building of it.

When you study the Tabernacle in the Wilderness beginning in **Exodus Chapter 25**, you will see that God laid out the plans for building it in extremely specific and minute details. This Tabernacle was God's design on earth of what many believe actually exists in Heaven today. It could be considered the "rough draft" of Solomon's Temple, Herod's Temple and the third temple that the book of Revelation tells us will, one day soon, be re-built. Today in Israel, the Wailing Wall is the last remaining remnant of Solomon's Temple of old and is the site for the future one to be built! The Tabernacle was how God chose to institute the sacrificial system of innocent animals covering man's sins. Those "coverings", through the various sacrifices, were a type of Christ sacrificing His life blood for the sin of the world.

For God did not send His Son into the world to condemn the world, but that the world through Him might be saved. He who believes in Him is not condemned, but he who does not believe is condemned already, because he has not believed in the name of the only begotten Son of God.
John 3:17-18

Why include the Tabernacle in this book? Because every part and parcel of the Tabernacle, and subsequent Temples, represents the One who someday would come, the Messiah, Jesus Christ. Starting with the entrance there was only *one way, one door*, *to* gain entry into the Tabernacle. Jesus said,

"I am the door: by me if any man enter in, he shall be saved, and shall go in and out, and find pasture."
John 10:9

When entering the Tabernacle in the Wilderness through its only door (a representation of Christ), they immediately encountered the brazen altar. On its north side was the area where the innocent animals were slaughtered by the Levitical Priests.

A man would bring a live, prescribed, perfect animal to be sacrificed for the atonement of his sins. In a ceremony of prayer, the priest would ask God to transfer the sins of the man into the animal. In turn, the innocence of the animal would be transferred onto the man covering his sins and those of his family for one full year. This would take place hundreds of thousands of times, so the people would find forgiveness with Almighty God.

Now, let me ask you a question. Were their sins forgiven for one year because of how strong their faith was in this process? Or, were their sins forgiven because of the completion of the work, the obeying of the law?

Let me put this to you another way. Prior to the law being given, while the children of Israel were slaves in Egypt, on the night of the Feast of Unleavened Bread, the first Passover, God told Moses to instruct the people to sacrifice a lamb. They were to paint the blood of the sacrifice on their door posts, tops and sides (up and sideways) so that it formed the shape of a Cross. (**Exodus 12:22**)

Was it the *faith* of the occupants inside the dwelling that saved them from the Angel of

Death? Or, was everyone inside saved because they *obeyed* the command? Everyone inside the residence was saved from the Angel of Death because they *obeyed* the command by being inside. Their *faith,* or lack of it, played no part in escaping the Angel of Death.

In like manner, the act of obedience of bringing the sacrifice to the Tabernacle cleansed the people of their sins for one year, but did not require faith. Nowhere in the Bible were the children of Israel REQUIRED to have faith in this process. Certainly, most of the participants had faith, but they had no tangible proof; only faith. This is why they obeyed. After all, this was the prescribed manner, the process that God ordained.

Throughout this entire book, I will never demean or marginalize your faith. In fact, the Bible says, "*that without faith it is impossible to please God.*" **Hebrews 11:6**

But, how much faith does it take to please God? And, what happens if my faith is not as strong as yours or if your faith is not as strong as mine? What if neither of us has enough faith to please Him? Do people who have more faith (or at least pretend to have more faith) get more blessings from God than you do? These are all questions I will attempt to answer as we continue through this book.

Let's get back to the Tabernacle in the Wilderness.

The Tabernacle in the Wilderness was built in precise and exact detail as per God's instructions. That is why it is no coincidence that the bronze laver (used for ceremonial cleansing) was built on the opposite side of where the sacrifices took place, opposite the door of entry. The brazen, or bronze laver, was the area for washing. However, the ceremonial washing took place after the sacrifice was made! The sacrifice was entirely consumed by fire and its ashes offered up for another portion of the ceremonial law.

The Bible says that the brazen laver, located west between the Altar of Sacrifice and the Altar of Incense, was east before the entrance of the Holy of Holies. It was filled with water for the cleansing of the Levitical Priests, typifying that they had been cleansed by the sacrifice and were now "washing with water". Today, its New Testament counterpart is found in Ephesians.

...that He might sanctify and cleanse her with the washing of water by the word, that He might present her to Himself a glorious church, not having spot or wrinkle or any such thing, but that she should be holy and without blemish.
Ephesians 5:25-17

As long as your Christian walk is in Christ, and you are drinking from the well of water that only He provides, as a Christian, you will never be thirsty!

Jesus answered and said to her, "If you knew the gift of God, and who it is who says to you, 'Give Me a drink,' you would have asked Him, and He would have given you living water."
John 4:10

The Bible says the laver was covered with polished mirrors. The Priests could see their own reflections as they came to be cleansed. When they walked away from the mirrors that comprised the brazen laver, their image in the mirror no longer remained. As long as you remain in Christ, as long as you continue to take of the water of life freely, your reflection remains. The minute you walk away, your reflection is gone. Today (in Christ), you are the Tabernacle of God. You take the Lord with you everywhere you go!

In the Tabernacle and subsequent Temples of God, the sacrifice was first, then came the washing with the water. This teaches us that when one enters the door (Christ), he or she does not clean up his or her act first and then come to the sacrifice which is Christ. You come to Christ first, and He cleanses you. The Holy Spirit in you does the cleansing, you simply receive!

"Come now, and let us reason together," says the LORD, "Though your sins are like scarlet, They shall be as white as snow, Though they are red like crimson, They shall be as wool."
Isaiah 1:18

As long as you remain in Christ, His righteousness continues to be YOUR righteousness, your cleansing. Although we are not taught this often, it is important for every Believer to own their righteousness in Christ. As an adopted son or daughter, you were freely given all the attributes of every Believer in the family of God! Those attributes include, but are not limited to, having free access to the Creator of the universe 24 hours a day, seven days a week. In fact, the Lord yearns to hear from us on a daily or even hourly basis!

The moment you accepted Christ as your personal Savior for the forgiveness of your sins, you acquired the righteousness of Christ. Believers today need to understand that their adoption by God was sealed and made permanent only by what Jesus did for them at the Cross, regardless of what level of faith you may or may not have. The love God has for you knows no bounds!

What is faith?

The biblical definition of faith is found in **Hebrews Chapter 11**, also known as the "faith chapter".

Now faith is the substance of things hoped for, the evidence of things not seen.
Hebrews 11:1

As with all of my teachings, I want to be as practical as I can and hope that the practicability of these teachings will turn into applicability in your everyday life! Most of us were taught that faith is a thing to be sought after. We were taught that we must strengthen our faith. Many pastors have described faith as muscles; the more you exercise your muscles, the more they grow. Obviously, the comparison is that the more your faith is exercised, the more it will grow. But this type of teaching lends itself to self-efforts and self-works. Allow me to explain.

When you look at faith as something to be achieved, you are already missing one of the foundational building blocks of God's message of GRACE. Faith, as an achievement or an accomplishment, is not New Testament faith at all. Yet, as with other biblical principles, the idea of our self-efforts, plans or schemes devised to strengthen our faith seems natural and correct. They are not!

Viewing faith as an achievement will cause a Christian to compare his or her faith to another. As a matter of fact, Paul warned us against that in second Corinthians.

For we dare not class ourselves or compare ourselves with those who commend themselves. But they, measuring themselves by themselves, and comparing themselves among themselves, are not wise.
2 Corinthians 10:12

When you begin to realize that faith is not something you achieve, but rather, it is something you receive from the Lord, you are on your way to understanding the message of God's GRACE. Think about the times that Jesus would correct his disciples by saying to them, "O ye of little faith." Was he chastising them for not believing hard enough? Was he concerned that their trust in Him was not sincere enough? Some of that may be true; however, what he was really saying is that you are not receiving enough of me to overcome the obstacles in your life. Your trust in ME is not sufficient to give you peace about whatever situation you are in. This is the lesson that we learn from the man who said "I do believe; help me with my unbelief."

Immediately the father of the child cried out and said with tears, "Lord, I believe; help me with my unbelief!"
Mark 9:24

It was only when the disciples came to the realization that they could not build their faith on their own that they made a simple request to Jesus, "Lord increase our faith"! **Luke 17:5**

As God himself continues to transform you from the inside out, you will realize that even your faith is to be received by God's GRACE. Although we have been taught differently, there is nothing we can do on the outside to strengthen our faith. Wait a minute! What about Bible reading? Doesn't reading my Bible increase my faith? Great question!

Yes, *faith comes by hearing and hearing the word of God.*
Romans 10:17

However, the reading of God's Word (the Bible) opens our eyes to the message of God's GRACE. That GRACE is poured out, over, and through every believer in direct proportion to how much you ask for it.

So, when it comes to building your faith the answer still remains the same. You must ask!

Having done nothing (except believe) to receive Christ, there is nothing that anyone can do to make Him leave.

For He Himself has said, "I will never leave you nor forsake you"...
Hebrews 13:5 (a)

You may ask, "Well, wait a minute." Don't I have free will? Yes, you do. You choose to accept Christ or not. Not choosing is to choose already. When you accept Christ as your Savior, He enters into your spirit, into your soul, into your heart of hearts. No actions, no law, no work that you did made you "born-again". It was done for you when you asked. Nothing you can do or say can reverse the process.

I explained it to our congregation like this. If you have ever been to New York in your lifetime, there is nothing you can do to "Un-York" yourself. There is nothing you can do to take back the fact that you had already been to New York. Obviously, there are people who have prayed a prayer, or filled out a card at some church, who will say they are saved. They then walk their own way, away from the Lord, never to grow or enjoy the blessings that only He can provide in their lives. They bear no fruit and show no sign of being "born-again".

Were these folks ever really saved in the first place? I don't think so.

Did they ever accept Christ into their hearts, or did they just mouth some meaningless words? We cannot judge. We can only assess their fruit or the lack of it.

I heard Pastor Joseph Prince explain it this way. He showed a video of an ounce of gold in his hand. He then took the ounce of gold and threw it in the mud so that the beautiful gold was now covered in mud. He then asked the question, "Did the piece of gold ever stop being gold?" No, it didn't!

Who shall separate us from the love of Christ? Shall tribulation, or distress, or persecution, or famine, or nakedness, or peril, or sword? As it is written: "For Your sake we are killed all day long; we are accounted as sheep for the slaughter." Yet in all these things we are more than conquerors through Him who loved us. For I am persuaded that neither death nor life, nor angels nor principalities nor powers, nor things present nor things to come, nor height nor depth, nor any other created thing, shall be able to separate us from the love of God which is in Christ Jesus our Lord.
Romans 8:35-39

In spite of being covered in the mud and muck (your sins), you never stop being His child. In spite of the fact of your sins and the subsequent condemnation that comes with acts of sin, you need to know that God never stops loving you! He never stops considering you His child. You can take great comfort in the fact that there is no longer any condemnation to those who are in Christ Jesus. **Romans 8:1**

Christ has redeemed us from the curse of the law, having become a curse for us. For it is written, "Cursed is everyone who hangs on a tree."
Galatians 3:13

The strength of sin is the law!

*The sting of death is sin, and the **strength of sin is the law**.*
1 Corinthians 15:56

That is a very confusing biblical statement. We know the law is good, right? So, how can the "strength of sin be the law"? Verse 56 in the Amplified Bible reads like this ... ***sin exercises its power upon the soul through the law.***

Is that hard to understand? How can the law produce sin? Paul put it this way,

I would not have known sin except through the law. For I would not have known covetousness

unless the law had said, "You shall not covet."
Romans 7:7(b)

Ah, are you starting to see it now? Or, are you still having trouble? Picture yourself driving down a very long, secluded road. It's a beautiful day. You can see for miles, and you are driving about 55 mph. In fact, there are no signs that tell you what the speed limit is. You continue to drive about 55 mph when all of a sudden you see those dreaded red and blue flashing lights in your rearview mirror. As that sinking feeling drops down into the pit of your stomach, you wonder why the policeman is pulling you over. After he asks for your license and registration, he then asks if you know why he pulled you over. In truth, you have no idea what you may have done wrong. To your surprise, he tells you that you were doing 55 in a 25 mph speed zone. What!? You have got to be kidding me! I did not see a single sign. You take your case to court pleading your case to the judge and truthfully stating that there were no speed signs! The judge carefully reminds you that ignorance of the law is no excuse. Guilty!

Now, this would be an absurd example unless you live in Arizona. Then, you know exactly what I'm talking about.

If the speed limit was properly posted for 25 mph, and you were doing 55 you were breaking the law. *"I would not have known sin except through the law..."*

Let's look at it another way because it is important that you understand why God produced the law. It was never meant for us to keep. It is a standard of perfection (the law is good) designed to specifically teach us how far short we come of it! Because of our Adamic, or sinful nature, our "flesh" constantly pulls us in the wrong direction, constantly pulls us towards sin.

Picture yourself in a circular room that has ten closed doors, and you are in the middle. Every one of the doors looks exactly alike. However, there is only one door that says, **Do Not Open**. What door will you naturally be inclined to look behind? Most of us are drawn to the things that we are not permitted to do: to lust after a woman that is not our wife, to be envious or jealous, to be like others or covet what our friends have, to take what we have not earned, to lie instead of facing reality. We all fall short of God's perfect standards, the law!

For all have sinned and fall short of the glory of God,
Romans 3:23

The strength of sin is the law! Do you get it now? That is the effect the law has on us, because we are a fallen species. It sets up a standard we can never attain because we are not perfect.

In the Garden of Eden, Adam and Eve were told that out of all of the trees in the garden, there was only one tree that they could not eat of, the tree of the **Knowledge** of **Good and Evil.** This was the only "law" they had to obey.

Throughout the centuries people have asked, "Why did God place that prohibited tree in the garden in the first place?" After all, if He would not have created that tree, Adam and Eve would not have been tempted to sin. Therefore, that would have saved the human race all of the misery we suffer at times because of the curse from God on us and the earth.

The answer should be obvious to most, but it is not. The answer is really very simple. Without the ability to choose, without the ability to "sin" or break the law, man could not have a free will. You were born with a free will. Without the opportunity to disobey, you and I are nothing but robots or zombies. We are made in God's image, not the image of robots or zombies.

Chapter 2

The Nature of Sin or The *Sin Nature*

Therefore, just as through one man sin entered the world, and death through sin, and thus death spread to all men, because all sinned.
Romans 5:12

The Sin Nature is that part of the essence of the soul acquired at Adam's fall in the Garden of Eden, and subsequently, passed on to **every person at birth**. **Genesis 6:5**

This is in direct opposition to the thinking of the world and sadly, the teaching of many churches today. The idea that all men and women are basically born "good" is in direct conflict with the teachings of the Bible. **Romans 3:10**

The Sin Nature has an "area" of strength in which human "good" is produced. They are those good deeds and thoughts which are acceptable to man and seem right in his eyes, but which are unacceptable to God, specifically for the purposes of salvation and spiritual growth.

Many Christians today believe that if something is "good", it must come from God. This is not necessarily the case. The same can be said of **truth.** All truth is not God's truth. It may be true that ancient Aztec civilizations used to sacrifice babies in fire ceremonies. But, that most certainly is not God's truth. Remember, we are talking about this tree of the knowledge of **Good** and **Evil**.

*And out of the ground the Lord God made every tree grow that is pleasant to the sight and good for food. The tree of life was also in the midst of the garden, and the tree of the knowledge of **good** and evil.*
Genesis 2:9

The root of the temptation that Satan used to convince Eve to eat the fruit of that tree was to make it appear that God was denying them something "good": "...you will be like gods..." **Genesis 3:5**

Then, Jesus went on to quote **Psalm 82:6:** ..."you are gods" and repeated that verse in **John 10:34** "...Is it not written in your law, I said, 'You are gods?'" However, He **never meant this as a good thing**!

The worst lies are those that contain some truth! In churches, very often there can be scriptures or sayings in the Bible **taken out of context**. It is not uncommon to hear Christians or even Pastors say these phrases:

All that is required is to love God with all your heart,

All you need is love,

Just love your neighbor as yourself,

You can't love God unless you love yourself, and so on.

In general, these philosophies and others like them contain *some* truth. They appear to be "GOOD". Remember, the tree in the garden that Adam was told not to eat was the Tree of

GOOD & **Evil.** As I heard a pastor once say, "When you take the **text** out of **context,** all that is left is the **con**!"

We know there is only one way for our faith to grow. The Bible says that it is through His Word, but it must be kept in context.

So then faith comes by hearing, and hearing by the word of God.
Romans 10:17

Many Christians today are making the mistake of living their Christian lives based on catchy phrases, catchphrases or easy to remember Bible verses.

An entire denomination came into existence based on taking the following verse out of context. Well-meaning "Christians" believe that by handling dangerous snakes they are exercising or proving their faith in God. This is an extreme example of taking a verse out of context, but we all know it to be real. Many men and women have been killed in this un-biblical practice.

Behold, I give you the authority to trample on serpents and scorpions, and over all the power of the enemy, and nothing shall by any means hurt you.
Luke 10:19

Taking Bible verses out of context is a critical mistake if you are going to learn to live for God. The worst thing you can do, or any teacher can do for that matter, is take a few verses out of context and build a doctrine on them. Yet, this is becoming more of the norm in Bible believing churches rather than actual verse by verse study holding true to the context. Remember, in learning the word of God, context is everything. For anyone to suggest, or to actually build their theology on a single verse, is what Jesus was referring to as building (their house) on sinking sand. Context is "king" with a small "k".

But everyone who hears these sayings of Mine, and does not do them, will be like a foolish man who built his house on the sand: and the rain descended, the floods came, and the winds blew and beat on that house, and it fell. And great was its fall.
Matthew 7:26

Think about what Jesus is saying. It seems simple, but unless you take a closer look, you can miss the deeper meaning. Jesus is the *rock*. We know this. He is the *rock* of our salvation. He is the author and finisher of our faith.

But what is sand? Sand is nothing more than tiny little pieces of rock. So, it is possible to build your doctrine on little pieces of truth, little pieces of sand; but little pieces of sand are not enough, and Jesus warned us that this is not something you can build your house, or your faith on! This is why Bible verses taken in proper context are so important to the Believer. Although I hate to see it, Bible verses taught in proper context are becoming rarer in Bible believing churches!

I heard a street preacher the other day say, *"The red letters of Jesus in the Bible are much more important than the words of Paul."* He was young, and I did not bother to correct him. The truth is that the red letters indicating what Jesus said were placed there by publishers as a marketing ploy to sell more bibles. The entire Bible is God's inspired, infallible WORD to us, regardless of what color the print is!

Man-made philosophies proclaimed as "good" have started to slowly creep into the church, replacing the gospel of Jesus Christ. This is not good! They have the appearance of being "good", they sound "good", they make people feel "good", but they are not the true gospel of Jesus Christ. Therefore, to the Believer they are NOT "good."

Today you can go into any Christian bookstore, and the bookshelves are inundated with "Christian" self-help books. There are books that purport to help a Christian grow closer to the Lord; help you with your temper, help you with your marriage, help you with your finances, help you with your healing. The list of "Christian" self-help books is endless.

Many Christians believe that man-made, man-centered, psychological or psychiatric philosophies covered in *"Christian-ease"* or Christian words make these man-made philosophies seem "Christian". So, therefore, these philosophies must be "good".

In reality, the core of all of these man-made teachings is that YOU have the power; YOU can achieve great heights; YOU can do it if only; YOU _____ (*fill in the blanks!*) Generally, it is *"you can do it, if you buy their book!"* When they teach that it is all about **YOU** and not about Jesus, run, run away as fast as you can!

The Bible is very clear.

But we are all like an unclean thing, and all our righteousnesses are like filthy rags; we all fade as a leaf; and our iniquities, like the wind, have taken us away. (from God-emphasis mine)
Isaiah 64:6

This is why Adam was told not to eat of the tree of the Knowledge of **Good** and **Evil**. In the Bible, human good is contrasted with divine good. Divine good is only produced by the Holy Spirit as a Believer looks towards Jesus Christ and what he did for them, personally, on the Cross. What Jesus did on the Cross for you was a finished work!

The Sin Nature also has areas of weakness which directs the production of all personal sin.

Hebrews 12:1 Three types of personal sin are produced here: mental attitude sins, sins of the tongue, and open, willful sinful activity. The Sin Nature produces patterns of lusts or desires, the basic motivators of all the activities of human life. The basic drives include the desire for power, ego satisfaction, sexual satisfaction, and material satisfaction, just to name a few.

The Sin Nature has a system of trends, or inclinations, which vary from person to person. Some people have an inclination toward immorality or lasciviousness. **Romans 1** Others have an inclination toward morality, or asceticism. These attributes all emanate from the Sin Nature, or the *ADAMIC* nature of Sin. **Romans 10:3**

Any trend in this regard is a product of the Sin Nature. The trends of the old (un-regenerated) Sin Nature are derived from the individual lust pattern(s).

But each one is tempted when he is drawn away by his own desires and enticed.
James 1:14

There are certain areas of our lives in which we may lust, and other areas where we may not. This is why one person may have a proclivity to become an alcoholic, and another person has absolutely no problem taking one or two drinks and then stopping. One person feels like they can't stop themselves from stealing, and another person has never been tempted to steal in entire their life.

The proclivities of the old Sin Nature come in two basic varieties: legalism and lasciviousness. Legalism, unrestrained, results in moral degeneracy. A person who is solely dependent upon his or her own "good" behavior may eventually substitute that outward behavior for righteousness which is only found in Christ. There is a distinct difference in being good FOR Christ and being good BECAUSE of Christ. Legalism will keep a man or woman "in-line" for short periods of time. Mere humans do not have the ability to keep the law or the rules permanently. In fact, most Christians cannot even keep the Ten Commandments. True righteousness is ONLY found in Christ.

Lasciviousness, unrestrained, results in immoral degeneracy: sexual perversion, pedophilia, and, at various times in human history, even human sacrifice.

Both trends in the old Sin Nature result in distortion and erroneous conclusions and beliefs. For example, moral strictness, with its self-righteousness and self-vindication, is often mistaken for the Christian way of life. People who are outwardly, morally strict are often considered to be great Christians. Their morality originates from outwardly obeying laws or rules that they or their church have established as the benchmarks which, in their opinion, make them good Christians.

In reality, the Christian way of life is a supernatural way of life and demands a supernatural means of execution. This is only accomplished by the Holy Spirit working on the inside of the person and not by their outward rule keeping or good works.

...For the Lord does not see as man sees, for man looks at the outward appearance, but the Lord looks at the heart.
1 Samuel 16:7(b)

There is also a distortion involving those with the trend toward lasciviousness. Christians say such a person cannot do "those *horrible* things" and still be a Christian. Immoral degeneracy, with its sexual sins, violence, terrorism, murder, and drug addiction, is construed as **not** being Christian. These are certainly not Christian attributes, but just as certainly, there are genuine Christians who struggle with these sins.

So, in the first distortion, people think you are "good" because you appear to live the Christian life. In the second distortion, people think that if you live a recalcitrant life, you're probably not a Christian at all. Legalistic shock in these cases draws one to conclude that it must have been a "head belief" and not a "heart of faith" belief.

Born-again Believers still possess an old Sin Nature and still commit sins. To deny such is to simply deny one's own reality in this world. Though saved, we remain human!

I once heard Pastor Prince explain it this way. If you get a clear glass of muddy water from a river, eventually the dirt will settle to the bottom of the glass. You will have clean, drinkable water at the top and dirt at the bottom. It will stay that way until you, or somebody, stirs things up! Although we all carry the dirt around, there is only one way to stop the stirring process in your life. Keep your eyes on what Jesus did for you, *personally,* on the Cross.

Therefore by the deeds of the law no flesh will be justified in His sight, <u>for by the law is the knowledge of sin</u>.
Romans 3:20

When I speak of the Cross, I am most certainly not talking about two pieces of wood! I am, in fact, referring to the willingness of Jesus to shed His blood, His obedience unto death, and the power of His resurrection! Your faith and acceptance in what He did allows the Holy Spirit the ability to work in your life.

What determines the reality of one's salvation is a personal faith in the Lord Jesus Christ, and what He did for you, personally, on the Cross, not the category of your sins. The Believer, out of fellowship with God, may actually commit any sin that his unbelieving counterpart would commit. Continued participation in sins as specified in **1 Corinthians 6:9-10 and Galatians 5:19-21** will ultimately determine whether a "Believer" was ever saved to begin with, or may result in his or her loss of salvation (depending on your theological point of view). **Romans 7:15**

As I teach in our church, no matter how someone gets to that point, whether saved or never saved in the first place, that person is in big trouble! That person's eternal soul hangs in the balance.

There are several terms used in scripture to refer to what is known as the Sin Nature or sin (in the singular). **Psalms 51:5, Romans 5:12, 7:14, 1 John 1:8**

Flesh - the emphasis here is on the bodily location of the Sin Nature, in the "flesh" or life of the individual. **Romans 8:8, 7:18, 13:14, Galatians 5:16-21, Ephesians 2.3**

Old Man - refers to the Believer's former manner of life as an unbeliever. **Ephesians 4:22, Colossians 3:5-9**

Heart - In some usages the word "heart" refers to a facet of the soul which is the source of sin. **Jeremiah 17:9, Matthew 12:34, 15:19, Mark 7:21-23, Psalms 58:2-5**

Carnality - derives from the Latin for "flesh". **Romans 7:14, 8:6-8, 1 Corinthians 3:1-3**

The Sin Nature is the source of spiritual death and is only kept at bay by the cleansing blood of Jesus; spiritually and purposely applied, daily, even hourly in one's life. **Romans 5:12, Ephesians 2:1, 5** The Sin Nature is perpetuated in human beings through physical birth. **Psalms 51:5, 1 Timothy 2:13, 14** The Believer continues to have a Sin Nature even after salvation. **1 Corinthians 3:1, 1 John 1:8** The Believer under the control of the Sin Nature is called "carnal". **Romans 7:14, 1 Corinthians 3:1**

The Sin Nature frustrates the work of the Holy Spirit and can only be tamed by placing one's faith exclusively in what Christ did for us on the Cross. This daily walk of faith must be applied on a daily or hourly basis. No church, pastor or priest can confer God's GRACE upon you. You must ask for it daily!

Give us this day our daily bread.
Matthew 6:11

No need to worry. The Sin Nature will NOT be found in the Believer's resurrected body. When we finally get to heaven, none of the cares of this world will be able to affect us!
1 Corinthians 15:56, Philippians 3:21, Colossians 3:4, 1 Thessalonians 5:23

God has arranged to provide all that is needed to deal with the problems caused by the Sin Nature in a Believer's life today. It is HIS GRACE! A Believer's righteousness is imputed by faith; never *earned*. The personal sins of the individual were borne by Jesus Christ on the Cross. **1 Peter 2:24** These sins will never be mentioned again because they have already been judged in Christ, wholly and completely!
Revelation 20:12. Psalm 103:12

The Bible clearly rejects man's "good" produced in his flesh. It is flatly rejected in terms of its use as "currency" to purchase salvation. **Ephesians 2:8, 9** This makes it clear that salvation can only be obtained by GRACE. The unbeliever will be at the Great White Throne of Judgment because he or she rejected God's GRACE (God's goodness) provided by His Son, Jesus Christ. **Revelation 20:11-15**

The Believer's sins were borne on the Cross by the Lord. **2 Corinthians 5:21** When a Believer commits a sin, Satan becomes his accuser. Jesus Christ is our Advocate. He pleads our case so much so that God declares the Believer RIGHTEOUS in Christ. There is a huge difference between a person being found *not guilty,* and a person being made **RIGHTEOUS!** Upon accepting Christ's atoning death for his or her sins, a Believer is made righteous! It is an **imputed** righteousness, but a righteousness imparted to every born-again Believer. ABSOLUTELY!

"Imputed" in the original Greek language is translated "*Logizomai*" Strongs Number 3049, an accounting term indicating your balance sheet is paid in full!

What about confession of sins?

Confession, in and of itself, is not where Believers gain their forgiveness. To true Believers, forgiveness was obtained at the

Cross by accepting what Christ did on that Cross for the personal forgiveness of their sins. He who knew no sin became sin for you.

Why confess at all? Specifically, in 1st John 1:9, that word confession in the Greek is the word, HOMOLOGEO Strongs Number 3670 (*hama-lay-gay-o*). It means to concede or agree with.

So, when a Believer confesses his or her sins, he or she is not telling God anything He does not already know. He or she is simply agreeing with God that what was done was a sin. This is why the actual act of CONFESSION does not forgive the Believer. The confession keeps the relationship in harmony. It is the price Christ paid on the Cross that secured the Believer's forgiveness.

This is similar to the old wives tale about two children walking home on an abandoned railroad track. Both their little legs had a difficult time walking over the stones and uneven railroad ties. One of the children found that they could go a little faster and their walk was a little easier, if they walked with one foot in front of the other on one of the tracks. However, because of lack of balance, they could not walk very far without falling off! The other child realized that if they held hands in the middle to help each other stay in balance, they could walk on the tracks much faster without falling off.

This is what confession does to your relationship with the Lord. It keeps you in balance. It keeps you in touch. It keeps you in fellowship. I reiterate, confession does not save you, nor is it a requirement for the Lord's forgiveness. He forgave you at the Cross for all your sins: past, present, and future. Confession simply keeps you in fellowship.

As stated earlier, human "good" is rejected by God. **Ephesians 2:8, 9** It is never acceptable to God, and it does not produce blessings in the life of the Believer. What most of us have not been taught is that the same GRACE that saves is the GRACE that keeps us. This is very different than what most of us have been taught in the past.

Most of you were taught that you are saved by grace and not of yourself. It is a gift from God! Of course, that is correct. However, without saying so, many Bible believing churches teach: *now that you are saved by grace get to work!* Get to work in the church nursery. Get to work helping in ministry somewhere, just get busy for the Lord and get to work. Bible believing churches roll out an endless list of rules that new believers can and cannot do. The message of God's Grace and God's goodness gets diluted and eventually gives way to "good works" and more "good works." No wonder so many well-intentioned Believers give up and walk away. They find themselves failing at keeping up with all the "good works" that they feel obligated to do. They find themselves failing at keeping the law. Why? It is because most of this is done in their own strength and their own intellect.

Most of us were taught that the more we perform "good things," the more God is pleased with us. This is contrary to the principle of GRACE, in which God does the work for the Believer. In Christian growth, the Holy Spirit provides for the production of divine good in Believers' lives, as they express their faith exclusively in what Christ did for them at the Cross on a daily basis. **Luke 9:23** Though counterintuitive to our human nature, God does the giving: man does the receiving.

Legalism is the human production of man-made "good" for the purpose of earning and receiving merit or blessings from God. Often times, new Believers may be told what to wear or what not to wear; where they can go, or where they can't go; what they can eat and drink, or what they can't eat and drink. The Believers then develop a false sense of security in thinking that as long as their behavior remains within those false parameters, they are a "good" Christian. Of course, the opposite is believed when they fall outside of those false parameters. In Legalism, man does the work and receives the credit. Therefore, Legalism is also a product of the Sin Nature. Although they will not lose their salvation, "keeping the rules" is described in the Bible as "wood, hay, and stubble". However, work done by the Holy Spirit will remain.

For no other foundation can anyone lay than that which is laid, which is Jesus Christ. Now if anyone builds on this foundation with gold, silver, precious stones, wood, hay, straw; each one's work will become clear, for the Day will declare it, because it will be revealed by fire, and the fire will test each one's work, of what sort it is. If anyone's work which he has built on it endures, he will receive a reward. If anyone's work is burned, he will suffer loss: but he himself will be saved, yet so as through fire.

1 Corinthians 3:11-15

Being "born-again" is the only way Jesus taught us to have a new spirit. This is why Jesus said, ...you must be born-again."

John 3:7

Your sinfulness, or the part of you that draws you toward sin, can only be changed by asking Christ into your heart, into your spirit. The Catholic Bible says *you must be born from above* (you must be born-again). This is a spiritual work that God does in the life of all who accept and believe.

When one becomes born-again, God begins a transformation in our lives. This is a process known as sanctification.

For the law was given through Moses, but GRACE and truth came through Jesus Christ.
John 1:17

Chapter 3

Spiritual Growth

*There is therefore now **no condemnation** to those who are in Christ Jesus, who do not walk according to the flesh, but according to the Spirit. For the law of the Spirit of life in Christ Jesus has made me free from the law of sin and death. For what the law could not do in that it was weak through the flesh, God did by sending His own Son in the likeness of sinful flesh, on account of sin...*
Romans 8:1-3

In Matthew Chapter 9, Jesus spoke about putting new wine into old wineskins. The simple implication was that the religious leaders of the day were immersed in the Law and they were so engrossed in their religious, legal positions that they were not able to assimilate any of Christ's teachings. Their religious, dogmatic ways of thinking about God left no room for the New Testament or its covenant teachings. If we are not careful, we can become old wineskins ourselves. Thinking that we know it all and that there is nothing left in the Bible for us to learn!

As you read in Romans chapter 8, the Bible is very clear. There is **NO condemnation** for those who are in Christ Jesus. That's not up for interpretation. **No condemnation** means just that, **NO condemnation**. This is why those who would have you believe that born-again Christians must keep or obey any part of the law, simply do not understand the new covenant. You have been forgiven. Own that fact!

As I said earlier, the Law is good. However, the Law, or religion, makes demands on an individual. Christians are not under the Law, but under GRACE which is God's unmerited favor, His unmerited, unending supply. There is a reason why God told Moses to put the Ten Commandments (the two tablets of stone) under the Mercy seat in the Tabernacle. The blood poured out on the Mercy seat which covered the Law in the Old Testament. Christ's blood shed for you in the New Testament covers the Law for you, once and forever. Jesus kept the Law in your place!

The work that Jesus did on the Cross needs nothing to be added. It was a finished work! If new covenant Believers were expected to keep the Law, then they were implying that Christ's work was not sufficient or complete. In other words, it is as if they are saying that we must add our "law keeping," or "good works" to the finished work of Christ on the Cross. It is biblically irrational, but that is exactly what modern day teachers of the Law are doing.

No, my friend, nothing needs to be added to the finished work of Christ. That is why the Bible teaches that there is no condemnation for those of us that are in Christ. When you were saved, you were born-again. All of your sins, past, present, and future, were paid for by Jesus.

Armed with this knowledge, by faith, we can be assured that our imputed righteousness given to us by Christ is sufficient. This negates the need to do penance or punish ourselves for our sins. Jesus already handled that! Now, before I go any further, I realize that some will say that I am giving Christians license to sin. This is the most common criticism of the GRACE message. Nonsense! God's view about sin has not changed one bit! Not once will you read or hear me say that Christians can sin with impunity because of God's grace. The Apostle Paul addressed this specifically:

What shall we say then? Shall we continue in sin that GRACE may abound? Certainly not!...
Romans 6:1-2

The classic teaching about sin and condemnation comes from Jesus, Himself. In

John Chapter 8, the religious leaders of the day brought a woman to Jesus who was caught in the very act of adultery. As Pastor Prince said, "The last time I checked, the act of adultery took two. Where was the man?"

The Pharisees, the religious leaders, thought they had Jesus trapped. They demanded to know what he would say about this woman. Stone her as the Law demanded or free her as HIS message of GRACE, love and peace was being taught?

Most of you know the story. Jesus said nothing at first. He simply stooped down to the ground, and with his finger, he began to write in the ground. He did so as though he did not hear them. **John 8:1-12**

Many have speculated as to what Jesus may have written on the ground. Whatever it was that Jesus wrote, and however he may have written it, got the attention of this poor woman's accusers. One by one they began to leave the scene until no one was left but this woman and Jesus.

Can you imagine the bewilderment of this woman as she looked up at Jesus, seeing all of her accusers gone and wondering what this incredible man of God would say? He simply asked her, "Where are those who condemn you? Where are your accusers?" She said,

"They are gone, Lord", and He said, "I do not condemn you either. Go and sin no more." **This is the quintessential message of God's GRACE to us!**

"Come now, and let us reason together, says the Lord: Though your sins are like scarlet, they shall be as white as snow; Though they are red like crimson, They shall be as wool."
Isaiah 1:18

Many of us have the wrong idea about God. We think we must clean up our act first and then come to God. This is the exact opposite of the truth. Jesus accepted this woman caught in the very act of adultery, forgave her and then told her to go and sin no more.

Just as I explained in the last chapter, Jesus cleans up our dirt, our sin, our "act" first. He makes us clean, forgives our sins and then gives us the strength to "sin no more".

If you're going to learn from this book, you are going to need to take ownership of the biblical fact that your sins are forgiven! You have been made a new person by accepting what Jesus did for you, personally, on the Cross. You need to remind yourself of this constantly and continually. You are righteous in the eyes of God, not by anything you do or don't do but, by exercising your faith daily, perhaps even hourly. What Jesus did for you makes you righteous.

Acceptance of that fact by faith makes you clean in the eyes of God.

You picked up this book because you have a sincere desire to draw closer to God. Our flesh and natural instincts tell us that we can only draw closer to God through our good works or our performances. This is not biblically correct. You are <u>made pleasing</u> to God only by what Jesus did for you on the Cross.

Our natural inclination in our flesh is to punish ourselves when we do wrong or when we sin. Often times, we will beat ourselves up for a certain amount of time until in the back of our minds, we feel like we have chastised ourselves enough. This is the condemnation that we heap upon ourselves, which is not of God and does nothing to help us understand our adoption and righteous position in Christ.

Still others, many of them Christians, are only too happy to help us with this vicious, unbiblical, and unholy cycle of condemnation that creates a barrier between us and God. The guilt and shame that we naturally feel for the things we do wrong cause us to run and hide from God. Adam experienced this in the garden.

Then the Lord God called to Adam and said to him, "Where are you? "So he said, "I heard your voice in the garden, and I was afraid because I was naked, and I hid myself." And

He said, "Who told you that you were naked?
Have you eaten from the tree of which I
commanded you that you should not eat?"
Genesis 3:9-11

Now, of course, God knew where he was
physically. God wasn't asking Adam what was
his geographical location. God was asking
Adam - What is your state of mind? What are
you thinking? Why is your heart removed from
me?

We do the same thing when we are ashamed
of our sin. When we do not comprehend God's
mercy and GRACE, like Adam, we go and hide.
Remember, Jesus said, "Neither do I condemn
thee, go and sin no more." God's mercy keeps
us from receiving what we all justly deserve;
an eternity in hell. God's Grace is continually
giving us what we have not earned; His
goodness!

Perhaps now you are starting to understand
how important it is for a Believer, if he wants
to live for God, to accept by faith his or her
position of righteousness in the eyes of God.
Where are YOU today? Are you trusting, in
spite of your failings, that God still loves you?
Are you trusting that God does not condemn
you? Or, are you trying to hide your heart from
God? Are you staying away from church;
staying away from fellowship with fellow
Believers?

When you understand that your adoption as a child of God is secure, you will not run and hide. You will learn to bask in His mercy and forgiveness! Nothing about basking in God's goodness and mercy will cause you to want to return to the pigpen of sin!

Again, many will say that this simply gives people license to sin. I cannot emphasize enough how incorrect this is. The idea that we can continue in sin so that God's GRACE and forgiveness will abound in our life is an anathema to God! It is an insult to your own intelligence. As a pastor said, "nobody puts on a new dress or a new shirt just to go play in the mud!!!" Sinning just to be forgiven is like going to jail just to take a shower! Who does that?

When you walk in the righteousness of Christ, understanding and appreciating the price He paid for your sins, you will not want to purposely return to the pigpen of sin! Those that do continue in their sin as a lifestyle with no remorse, were never really saved by Jesus in the first place. They did not truly accept His work on the Cross!

Moreover the law entered that the offense might abound. But where sin abounds, GRACE abounded much more,
Romans 5:20

"Where sin **abounds**" (*Pleonazo* in the Greek), GRACE **abounded** much more"
(*Huperperisseuo* in the greek) Super Abounds.
Strongs numbers 4121 and 5248

Natural GRACE **/ Super Natural GRACE!**
Greek Scholar, Kenneth Wuest puts it this way, "Where sin exists in abundance, GRACE is in SUPER abundance, and then more GRACE on top of that!" THAT'S POWERFUL!

In other words, wherever there is sin in your heart or in the world, there is more GRACE to cover that sin. In fact, Paul tells us in Romans that wherever sin is, there is more than enough GRACE to cover that sin, and even more GRACE than that!

Pastor Prince taught it this way, and it is a great example:
Scientists tell us that the earth only uses a tiny fraction of the radiant heat of the sun. The rest of the heat is dispersed throughout the universe! We only need a fraction of the heat from the sun to live. Yet God supplies that heat and GRACE to cover your sin in over abundant supply. This is why God tells us no matter how bad things get, there is a *Huperperisseuo SUPER* amount of God's GRACE to cover those sins. This is why the Bible teaches that we are **more than** conquerors!

> *Yet in all these things we are more than conquerors through Him who loved us.*
> **Romans 8:37**

Chapter 4

Precept upon Precept

*But we all, with unveiled face, beholding as in
a mirror the glory of the Lord, are being
transformed into the same image from glory to
glory, just as by the Spirit of the Lord.*
2 Corinthians 3:18

What does the passage above mean when it
says, "but we all, with unveiled face..."? Put
simply, the veil between us and God that
separated us from God has been removed. We
no longer need a priest (or Saints, if you are
Catholic) to make intercession for us. Why?
The reason being our Great High Priest, Jesus,
is ever making intercession for us. **Romans
8:34**

In other words, you can speak to God through
Jesus anytime, anywhere. He is omnipotent
and omnipresent. He hears everything and can
be everywhere at the same time. He even
knows your thoughts and knows what you

have need of before you even ask. **Matthew 6:8**

As you ask Him and invite Him to become more a part of your life, He will shape you and mold you and make the changes in your life that bring you happiness, peace, and rest! As I said earlier, the fancy word for that process is *sanctification*.

The process of *sanctification* **should** take place throughout the life of a Believer down here on earth. I use the word ***should*** because far too many Christians have convinced themselves that they have reached a point in their Christian lives where they cannot learn anything anymore! They may have been in Christian churches for many years. They may have read their Bible cover to cover many times. If a Believer thinks that he or she have seen and heard it all, they are already on the slippery slope of becoming an old wine skin. **Mark 2:22**

Thinking there is nothing else to learn as a Christian opens the door is the sin of *pride*. Those that think they know it all are those individuals that often times become the Christians that are the most critical of other Christians, pastors, or even books like this. Critical Christians, those who are looking to find fault with every teacher or every teaching, have become non fruit bearing Christians. They do not bare good fruit anymore because they are too busy finding things wrong with others.

The minute you stop growing as a Christian, you will start to go backwards!

If the Spirit of Christ is in you and you truly were born-again, that Spirit in you becomes more and more a part of you from the inside. As you surrender more of yourself, more of your flesh, more of the need to have things done your way, you give the Holy Spirit more latitude to grow and occupy more of your life. "More of You and Less of Me" (written by Nina Keck, copyright 2014) is one of my favorite Christian songs of all time. In fact, if our church in Southern Arizona has a theme song, that's it!

Remember, the process of becoming set apart for God, more Christ-like and holy, is the process of *sanctification*. Most of us have been taught that this holiness, this *sanctification*, is achieved by works or good behaviors. It's only natural to think that if I do certain things, or if I don't do other things, God will be pleased with me. Without realizing it, pastors and Christians that teach good behaviors as a means to gain holiness are teaching the Law. This is the "milk" of the Word and not the "meat" of the Word as taught by the Apostle Paul. Holiness is NOT the way to get to God. We get to God through Jesus, who makes us Holy! I will have more on that later.

As a Believer, the Light (Christ) that is now dwelling within you, as long as you are down here on this earth, is surrounded by your flesh. Light is always capable of dispelling darkness. However, our fleshly bodies become an obstacle to this Light and its ability to shine through.

Nor do they light a lamp and put it under a basket, but on a lampstand, and it gives light to all who are in the house.
Matthew 5:15

Although we may not fully understand how this process works, the good news is, it does work! If there is any secret to learning how to live for God and allowing the Holy Spirit to work and grow in your life, it is this - simply ask!!!! Keep your eyes on Jesus remembering always what He did for you, personally, on the Cross. It is the Lord, Himself, who actually does the work.
Matthew 21:42

If you then, being evil, know how to give good gifts to your children, how much more will your heavenly Father give the Holy Spirit to those who ask Him!
Luke 11:13

It is the biblical obligation of every true Believer to let his or her Light shine, allowing the love of God to shine through them in a multitude of ways so that others may see God in them. Letting the Lord shine is not just so that non-believers will be drawn to Christ. It allows you, as the Believer, to fulfill the plan that God has for you and has for every one of us.

For I know the thoughts that I think toward you, says the Lord, thoughts of peace and not of evil, to give you a future and a hope. Then you will call upon Me and go and pray to Me, and I will listen to you. And you will seek Me and find Me, when you search for Me with all your heart.
Jeremiah 29:11-13

But we are all like an unclean thing, and all our righteousness's are like filthy rags; we all fade as a leaf; and our iniquities, like the wind, have taken us away.
Isaiah 64:6

As we willingly place every aspect of our lives and our being at the foot of the Cross, Jesus himself (through the Holy Spirit) begins the work of *sanctification* in you. You simply get in the way, or frustrate the GRACE of God, when you try to do things on your own. **Galatians 2:21**

If that last statement angers you or makes you think that I am teaching heresies, do yourself a favor and keep reading! The message of God's GRACE at work in a Believer's life is nothing new. The idea of being at rest in Christ is the actual gospel of God's GRACE taught by Paul throughout the entire New Testament.

In their old age, Abraham and Sarah were promised a child. Many years passed, and Sarah did not conceive. Perhaps out of frustration, or perhaps out of a desire to see God's will be done, Sarah told her husband Abraham to go into her servant Hagar's tent to bring forth a child. This was an acceptable custom of the day, but was not God's perfect will for the circumstances. Hagar did, in fact, conceive and later gave birth to Ishmael.

Many more years passed, and still Sarah had not conceived a child. Now keep in mind, God had promised them a baby. God is never slack concerning his promises! **2 Peter 3:9**

Approximately 14 years later, in her very old age, Sarah conceived, and Isaac was born.

The Bible says that Ishmael was conceived by the bondwoman, Hagar. Ishmael became a type of the Law, not the child of promise. He was the product of an act of the flesh.

On the other hand, Isaac (a type of Christ), was the child of promise and would go on to fulfill the many other promises of God, including making Abraham's seed as many as the stars in the sky.

Sadly, that one decision and act in the flesh, no matter how good the motives may have been, has resulted in struggle and turmoil in the world ever since. The children of Ishmael, by and large, are the origin of all Muslims in the world. The children of Isaac went on to form the 12 tribes of Israel. The children of those two individuals, the child of the flesh and the child of the promise, have hated each other and have been fighting each other ever since.

Think about this! Excluding the Gospels, a large percentage of New Testament teaching is not focused on evangelism, teaching people how to be born-again. I do not know what the actual percentage is. My guess is it is somewhere in the area of 95 to 98%. For arguments sake, let's just say 95%. So if 5% of the New Testament teaches us how to get saved, what does the other 95% of the New Testament teach? **It teaches us how to live for God!** Most of us were taught that we live for God. We gain God's favor by the good works that we do. This may be a "good" teaching for beginners, but it is not "MEAT" for a Believer who wants a victorious, consistent and godly lifestyle.

Most of the teaching in Bible believing churches today will wholeheartedly embrace the fact that you are saved by GRACE, and only GRACE, and teach that it is not of your works. So, they all agree that you are saved by GRACE, but once saved you have to get to "work" to keep God's GRACE? It makes no sense and is not the gospel of God's GRACE taught in the New Testament.

Still not convinced? Let me ask you this one question. If you are saved by GRACE and kept by your works, why would you need to rely on Christ's death anymore after you got saved? What good does Christ's death, burial, and resurrection do for the Believer? The answer should be obvious - Everything!

The Message of the Cross is foolishness to those who are perishing, but to us who are saved it is the power of God.
1 Corinthians 1:18

The New King James puts it this way, *"For the message of the Cross is foolishness to those who are perishing, but to us who are **being saved** it is the power of God."*

Why did the translators do that? Why did the Bible scholars use the words **being saved**? They understood that in this powerful verse was the explicit implication of the sanctification process, the ongoing work of the Holy Spirit in the life of every Believer every day!

We are going to look at many other verses on this topic, but let me ask you about this one verse in 1st Corinthians Chapter 1, Verse 18. What part do you play? What work do you have to do? How do you receive the power of

God through the Cross? The answer should again be obvious, but it is not. **You receive the power of God by faith!** It has nothing to do with your works and everything to do with the work of the Holy Spirit.

For what does the Scripture say? "Abraham ***believed God****, and it was accounted to him for righteousness."*
Romans 4:3

Are you catching on? It was not the fact that Abraham was physically willing to sacrifice his son Isaac. It was his *faith*. It was not the fact that Abraham had communion and paid tithes to Melchizedek. It was Abraham's belief, his faith in God that made him righteous. It is your faith in Christ and what he did for you on the Cross that makes YOU righteous.

As I said earlier, we simply get in the way and frustrate the GRACE of God when we try to do things ourselves for Him. Abraham learned this when he went to Hagar, and Ishmael was conceived.

Jesus said, *"For my yoke is easy and my burden is light."* **Matthew 11:30**

When you begin to fully appreciate God's GRACE in your life, you will begin to also appreciate that Jesus, Himself, sticks closer than a brother. **Proverbs 10:24 (b)**

By placing your faith in nothing more and nothing less than Jesus and what he did for you at the Cross, you are now, by faith, flowing in the *Dunamis* **Strongs Number 1411** (Doo-nah-miss) power of His resurrection! *Dunamis in the Greek is where we get our English word, dynamite! POWERFUL!*

As you submit to Jesus by way of His Cross, He changes you from the inside! That initial Light of the Holy Spirit that entered into you at your conversion begins to grow and show. The difference now is that He is the one sanctifying you, not your good works or your behaviors.

When we understand and accept the fact that all we receive from God is from His GRACE, we begin to understand that He, and He alone, makes the changes in our lives. All of these changes, all of the power to work miracles in our lives are all possible because of the finished work of the Cross!

Perhaps you are saying to yourself, I know Pastor Steve, but the Bible is very clear,

... If any man will come after Me, let him deny himself, and take up his Cross daily, and follow Me.
Luke 9:23

Do you remember I told you earlier how context is so important?

Let's put that verse in proper context. "....**let him deny himself**..." Most of us have been taught that in one form or another Jesus was teaching us asceticism as a prerequisite to being His disciple. In other words, the more I deny myself worldly pleasures and the more I deny myself in a sacrificial manner, the closer I will be to God. This entire line of thinking runs contrary to the New Testament. Yet, it is a teaching that many of us have wrongfully embraced for far too long! The dictionary describes asceticism as, "the doctrine that a person can attain a high spiritual and moral state by practicing self-denial, self-mortification, and the like." **dictionary.reference.com**

Do you really think that Jesus was teaching us to practice asceticism in order to be His disciple? If you think that teaching is correct, then your closeness to Christ is now dependent on your works, your actions, and your performance.

For they being ignorant of God's righteousness, and **_seeking to establish their own righteousness_**, *have not submitted to the righteousness of God.*
Romans 10:3

The story goes that a national magazine author was interviewing a monk living in a Catholic order way up in the mountains of France. To show their dedication to God, these monks lived the most circumscribed lives. One monk showed the author a carved out cave where he slept at night with one blanket, no pillow, and a small *sterno* canned flame for heat in the winter. The author was in awe of how much sacrifice this man of God, and these monks lived for their faith. The author, in awe, said to the monk, "This is amazing. You must feel so much closer to God than the rest of us." The monk replied, "Not really."

Our "works" do not bring us closer to God. Our righteousness through Jesus and our relationship with Him making us righteous is what pleases God.

What is the righteousness of God? It is the righteousness **provided for you** by the finished work of the Cross! Your righteousness is not your own. It does not come about by anything you do or don't do, by anywhere you go or don't go, by anything you wear or don't wear. Your righteousness was and is only established in what Jesus did for you at the Cross. He made you righteous! Once again, it is known as "imputed righteousness".

By denying that anything outside of the Cross of Christ can set you free from a sinful habit causes you (in a spiritual sense) to take up your Cross. Your continual identification with what Christ did for you on the Cross is how you *carry* it. You *carry* it with you by faith, twenty-four hours a day, seven days a week! No physical act, no matter how well motivated or thought out it may be can replace what Jesus did for you personally! Jesus was not saying, "I carried the Cross this far, now you carry it the rest of the way!" His last words were "**IT IS FINISHED!**"

As we will see by continuing to learn this teaching, the GRACE that saved you is the same GRACE that will keep you. The victorious Christian life is not a result of your actions, the things you do, or the things that you don't do. Just as your salvation was guaranteed and secured by GRACE through the Holy Spirit, your spiritual growth is accomplished by the same Holy Spirit. But, you must ask in order to receive! *Yet you do not have because you do not ask.* **James 4:2 (b)**

Chapter 5

The Jesus Cycle!

As I said earlier, I am amazed at the number of Bible churches and Bible believing pastors who teach and believe that we are saved by GRACE, and only GRACE, and that not of our works. Then, they turn around and teach now that we have been saved by GRACE, we need to **get to work** *so that God will be pleased with us*. It makes no sense. Yet, I believed that way and taught that way for many years. I simply did not understand God's Goodness towards us!

When the disciples came to Jesus and asked Him to teach them what they should do that they might work the works of God, Jesus answered them plainly.

*Jesus answered and said to them, "This is the work of God, **that you believe** in Him whom He sent."*
John 6:29

That's Jesus, folks! Whom He sent is Jesus! The only part that we play in doing the work of God is to **believe**. This is done by faith and not by our works, no matter how good those works may be. Are you saying that my works for God have no part in my relationship with Him? I did not say that. But again, I want to ask you, "What works did you do to be saved?" The answer is none. It was only by *faith* that you accepted the fact that Jesus forgave you of your sins personally. It is only by faith in what Christ did at the Cross that brought about salvation in your life. So, are you saying we are saved by GRACE and kept by works? Of course not. Once again, the same GRACE that saved you is the same GRACE that keeps you.

What about in James where it says *faith without works is dead*? That's a great question. I get that one all the time!

Let me reiterate, as I will do often in this book, context is everything. Let's look at that verse more closely. The Bible says:

> *Thus also faith by itself, if it does not have works, is dead.*
> **James 2:17**

Is the faith spoken of here a result OF the works? Of course not. So the faith is already standing; it's already in place. This verse was written to Believers who already have their faith in proper perspective in their lives.

Now the 18th verse goes on to say:

But someone will say, "You have faith, and I have works. Show me your faith without your works, and I will show you my faith by my works."
James 2:18

Did you catch that last part? "*...I will show you my faith by my works.*"

This has absolutely nothing to do with YOU acquiring Salvation or YOU producing Sanctification in your life. We do not "work" to stay in God's good graces or to gain His approval. His approval of you comes because of Jesus in you. Nothing needs to be added to the finished work of Christ.

Jesus said, "*Even so, every good tree bears good fruit, but a bad tree bears bad fruit.*"
Matthew 7:17

He did not say "many" or "most" trees bring forth good fruit. All good trees bring forth good fruit! The greater teaching here, of course, is that you as a born-again Believer, who has newness of the Spirit, must be producing good fruit. Our logical mind or our reasoning, our intellect, tells us that this fruit can only be produced through our good works, through our hard work. Again, this is what most of us have been taught all of our Christian lives. It is not the teaching of the Bible.

"For My thoughts are not your thoughts,
Nor are your ways My ways." says the Lord.
Isaiah 55:8

If you have a fruit tree planted in your backyard and it has been well fertilized, watered, well taken care of and receives just the right amount of sunlight, it will produce fruit. That is a fact of Dendrology (the study of trees in nature). Now, this may sound silly, but I assure you, the tree does not stand there constantly working and trying to squeeze out fruit! It is because it is well-fed and well-grounded that the natural process of producing fruit takes place. So, it is the same with you as a Believer. The more you water your roots by reading and studying the word, the more good fruit you produce.

...that He might sanctify and cleanse (you) with the washing of water by the word.
Ephesians 5:26

The more you grow closer to the **S O N,** not the S U N, the more fruit the Holy Spirit will produce through you!

Reading your Bible is to your spirit what eating food is to your body. Without a regular course of Bible reading, your spirit will get weaker and weaker. If you are a new Believer, I always recommend you start in the Gospel of John, and then go back to the first book of the New Testament, Matthew. This will give you a rooted and grounded basic understanding of the teachings of Jesus and how it applies to your daily life.

Draw near to God and He will draw near to you. Cleanse your hands, you sinners, and purify your hearts, you double-minded.
James 4:8

The more you read your Bible and ask and trust the Lord, the more you will produce good fruit, effortlessly! Your life will display a constant production of good fruit, **effortlessly!**

Now, skeptics will try to convince you that I am teaching you to simply sit on the couch and eat potato chips while God does everything for you. This is <u>not</u> what I am teaching, and it certainly is <u>not</u> what the Bible teaches.

*Now to him who **works**, the wages are **not counted** as GRACE but as debt. But to him **who does not work** but believes on Him who justifies the ungodly, **his faith** is accounted for righteousness, just as David also describes the blessedness of the man to whom **God imputes righteousness <u>apart from works</u>**:*
Romans 4:4-6

As you walk through your daily life down here on earth and the more you invite the Lord to be involved in your daily affairs, the more you will be able to stand back and watch the miracle of the Lord producing good fruit in your life. Asking God for wisdom, praying for your enemies, asking Him to intervene in every aspect of your life, trusting Him for guidance, blessings, peace, and stability, that is the biblical standard chosen by God for us!

The mistake many churches make is placing too much emphasis on a person's physical, educational, or natural abilities. Were you once a teacher? You should be working in the church nursery. Are you a handyman or a maintenance man? Then, do that work for your church or go to some foreign land and help build a church or school for orphans. You have a knack for organization? Well, the ushers and greeter ministries are probably for you!

There is nothing wrong with doing any of these works, but where we go off course is that after a certain amount of time of doing these things, these works can begin TAKING THE PLACE of our personal, intimate relationship with Christ.

Take a look at Psalm 23, which is just one of the many chapters in the Bible where God encourages his children to rest. The biblical word for *rest* is synonymous with the word **trust**!

First let me show you something you may have never considered.

The Lord is my shepherd; I shall not want. He makes me to lie down in green pastures: He leads me beside the still waters. He restores my soul: He leads me in the paths of righteousness.
Psalm 23

Who is doing the shepherding here, you or the Lord? Obviously, the Lord is your shepherd. How much should you need or want? The answer is none. **You shall not want**! At this point, if you just read that and think that I am referring to greed or selfishness, you are missing the whole point! I am sorry, but you just flunked the test! ☺

The Jesus cycle

When the Bible says, "You shall not **WANT**" it means that you shall not **LACK**, *CHACER* in Hebrew **Strongs Number 3670** (*Khaw-sare*). God is a very real and very loving God. He wants what is best for you and HE wants to supply ALL of your needs. He will, in direct proportion to how much you ask Him. He does, even when we forget to ask. But, the more you ask Him, the more He does. The more He does, the more you should thank Him. The more you thank Him, the more He will do for you! I call this the "**Jesus cycle**", and it is a marvelous way to live your life as a Believer!

Who makes you to lie down? Who makes you to rest? Not only does the Lord lead you to rest, but He makes sure that you rest in *"green pastures"!!!* He does not lead you to rough seas or rocky shores but to *"still waters"*. He restores your soul. He leads you in the path of righteousness. Who is supposed to be doing the leading? Who is supposed to be doing the restoring? It is not you!

To this day, I still cannot figure out why the 23rd Psalm is read out loud at so many funerals? This Psalm written by David is full of life and advice from God to help the readers have the abundant life that Jesus talked so much about.

Come to Me, all you who labor and are heavy laden, and I will give you rest.
Matthew 11:28

There are so many examples in the Old and New Testaments where God is constantly and continually trying to teach us to rest; to trust and to place our faith in Him and His desires for our lives. While the disciples were on the sea and the waves started roaring and the wind started howling, the natural, immediate reaction of the disciples was to row the boat faster; try harder and put more effort into their work. Instantly, Jesus calmed the waters and the wind. The Gospel of John tells us that they immediately found themselves at the safety of the shore. Let Him calm the storms in your life!
John 6:21

The idea of resting and trusting the Lord permeates the entire Bible! In the book of Ruth, Naomi tells Ruth concerning Boaz (another type of Christ known as the Kinsman Redeemer) to rest while the Lord works out her problems for her.

*Then she said, "**Sit still**, my daughter, until you know how the matter will turn out, for the man will not rest until he has concluded the matter this day."*
Ruth 3:18

Sitting still, being patient, resting, trusting; these things go against our flesh! Our flesh (our natural selves) wants to take control, turn the knobs and pull the levers in our lives! This is the exact opposite of living a life in Christ as a true Believer!

Nowhere in this book will I ever suggest that you simply lie on the couch and do nothing all day long! God does not work in our lives to make us lazy. However, as you learn to trust the Lord on a daily basis and learn to ask Him to guide your paths, to lead you to the right people, or the right job, or the right building, He will! The Lord waits patiently for us to invite Him to become more a part of our daily lives. The more we are willing to surrender to Him, the more He is willing, by His GRACE, to pour out His blessings over and through us, but we must ask! As one pastor put it, "When you work, God rests. If you rest, God works."

If you then, being evil, know how to give good gifts to your children, how much more will your Father who is in heaven give good things to those who ask Him!
Matthew 7:11

Years ago when our church was very small, a man who had recently given his heart to Christ gave a testimony in church. He went on about all the changes that were taking place in his life. All of us who were in the room that day identified with what he was saying and were full of joy for him, appreciating that another brother had been brought into the kingdom of God.

I'll never forget the last thing he said when he finished giving his testimony. He said, "Jesus has done so much for me. I am going to spend the rest of my life paying Him back." In our flesh, that sounds correct. It rings true, but it is not biblical! The truth is that we can never pay Jesus back for what He did for us on that Cross. This is not to say that we do not do good works for the Lord. We do. But, we do not do good works for the Lord to pay Him back. After conversion, the work that we do as a Believer for the Lord must come as a result of what has taken place in our lives. In other words, our good works will be the fruit of our daily lives, never the root!

Chapter 6

Let HIM Work, You Rest!

Therefore, since a promise remains of entering His **rest,** *let us fear lest any of you seem to have come short of it. For indeed the gospel was preached to us as well as to them, but the word which they heard did not profit them: not being mixed with faith in those who heard it. For we who have believed do enter that rest, as He has said: "So I swore in My wrath, they shall not enter My rest," although the works were finished from the foundation of the world."*
Hebrews 4:1-3

Throughout this book, I will be talking about resting in the Lord. As I said, when I mentioned the *rest* given to us by the Lord, it *does not mean inaction*. For the purposes of our teaching, the word rest is synonymous with *trust*. For many years, pastors (including myself), have taught men and women who struggle with learning how to live for God to simply work harder at the things they think will help them. Just as when they received the joy of their salvation, they probably took great pleasure in their "Christian disciplines". They instinctively began a "checklist" of "good things" that they should start doing or doing more of. Am I reading my Bible enough? Am I praying enough? Am I attending church enough? Am I paying my tithes? The list of Christian disciplines we have been taught we must do if we want to stay close to the Lord goes on.

Doing these things and others like them are very good. They are very natural and understandable. However, performing good works or trying to keep the Law does not keep you in right relationship with the Lord! As far as the New Covenant is concerned, they can be counterproductive and often lead to frustration, disappointment, and sometimes a failed faith!

It took me months to wrap my mind around these basic truths that I had overlooked all these years. I then began to try to comprehend this magnificent thing called **GRACE**. I started picking out all the man-made rules and laws I had created for myself. Am I praying enough? Am I reading my Bible enough? Am I Christ-like enough? Although my motives were good, I was looking for the answers in my own behavior, my own performance, and my own doings for the Lord.

Soon, I became comfortable with the idea of just how far-reaching the love of God is toward me. When I began to understand that love, and that it is completely a result of what Jesus did for you and me at the Cross, the Lord began to revolutionize my mind! Revival started taking place in my soul! My preaching and teaching began to take on the life of the Spirit, and my human failings were of no consequence anymore!

This is God's GRACE and mercy towards us! God's mercy is keeping us from receiving the punishment that we rightly deserve, and His GRACE is God giving us goodness that we do not deserve.

> *We love Him because* **He first loved us**.
> **1 John 4:19**

God's GRACE towards you is not limited to what you know intellectually. Many in the church today have a comprehensive, intellectual grasp of the principle of His GRACE. However, there is so much more!

Assimilating your knowledge of God's GRACE and having that knowledge move from your intellect or your mind to your heart is essential, if you are going to experience the freedom and victory found only in God's

GRACE. God's GRACE, which is made possible only by what Jesus did for you on the Cross. It was a finished work! It is all done by faith. You simply must believe and let the Holy Spirit do the work for you.

Although we discussed it before, let's go a little deeper into the following scripture.

*Then He said to them all, "If anyone desires to come after Me, let him deny himself, and take up his Cross **daily**, and follow Me."*
Luke 9:23

Too many of us have been taught that Jesus was trying to teach us that in order to be his disciple, we must be willing to give up everything, to lay aside everything in our lives, and take any punishment that comes our way. This supposedly becomes our Cross to bear. Somehow we believe that this will produce the victorious Christian life for us. Once again, this is not what Jesus was teaching. The idea that we must take up our Cross daily and suffer daily for the cause of Christ appeals to our flesh and makes sense to our intellect, but it is **biblically** incorrect!

This is where I begin to anger people. Nobody wants to be told that all of their hard work and determination in the name of the Lord does not lead to an abundant life full of victory for the Believer. Our genetic make-up, our flesh, better identifies with **cause and effect**. Do good, get good. Do bad, get bad. That is tangible. *(More on this in chapter 11)*

However, that is NOT the New Testament Gospel of God's GRACE! Most teachers will not admit it. They teach their congregations to work harder, try more, and pour more effort into living for God. It does not work. Certainly, our self-efforts can bring about short-term, short-lived temporary victories. A person may attend many self-help meetings every week or read the latest self-help book and that person may experience temporary victory. However, those who find any degree of "success" in programs, self-help books, other religions, or meditative techniques, must, of necessity, maintain a constant and continual vigil of such methods.

Again, the root of the "success" will be the result of a person's application, or their hard work, to make them successful. Quality of life "techniques" do not bring permanent change full of peace and tranquility as only Jesus can. In fact, many of these "practices" bring with them a plethora of anxiety and stress of maintenance and can have disastrous effects when not continually worked on or applied. Permanent change can only take place from the inside out, never the other way around. Trusting Christ for every aspect of one's life is the only way the Lord can make a permanent change and it is effortless!

But let's get back to taking up our Cross and following Jesus.

For me, it was the fact that Jesus said "daily". I am to take up my Cross daily and follow Him. I began to realize that, by faith, as I willingly placed every aspect of my life at the foot of the Cross, Jesus, Himself, through the Holy Spirit, began to make the changes in my life.

It is the Holy Spirit that will make the **PERMANANT** changes our lives. We simply get in the way. We frustrate the GRACE of God (**Galatians 2:21**) when we try to do things ourselves for God. Abraham learned this when he went to Hagar and Ishmael was conceived. Remember, *Jesus said, "… my yoke is easy and my burden is light."* When you begin to fully appreciate God's GRACE, you will realize that Jesus truly does stick closer than a brother.

So what does this have to do with taking up your Cross daily? By placing your faith in nothing other than the Cross of Christ, and what he did for you on that Cross, the verse above, and others like it, takes on a whole new meaning and begins to make more sense. Now, when I say the Cross of Christ, I am not talking about two pieces of wood or a piece of jewelry hanging around your neck or on your car's dashboard.

When I use the term *Cross* or *Cross of Christ,* I am referring to the willingness of Jesus to suffer and die for you. I am referring to the obedience of Jesus to ransom Himself and die as a sinless sacrifice for you. And, finally, the awesome, majestic power of the Holy Spirit at His resurrection! So when I say **the Cross,** it is the entirety of the **good news** of the **Gospel** of **Jesus Christ**.

As we submit to Him by faith, and to what the Cross means to all who will believe, He begins to actually change us from the inside. This is all done by faith. Faith in what He did for you at the Cross and believing it was a finished work!

Understand and accept the fact that we can receive nothing from God unless it is through His GRACE only made possible by the Cross, and that He, and He alone, frees us from the sins that hold us down. It gives a whole new meaning to what Jesus said in Luke Chapter 9 verse 23 when he said, "*take up your Cross daily….*"

Now, I hope you understand that by working harder or trying more, you don't make any **permanent** changes in your life. That is God's job! So when you take up your Cross and deny yourself, Jesus was not referring to asceticism. Remember, asceticism is the idea that a person can get closer to God through extreme abstinence, self-mortification, or rigorous self-denial. Asceticism, taken to its extreme by some, means that they will punish themselves physically in order to more clearly identify themselves with Jesus. No!

To reiterate, let that person **deny themselves.** Let them **deny** that anything in and of themselves or their actions, no matter how well motivated or thought out they may be, can bring them victory learning to live for God. God is not the taskmaster that others want to make Him out to be. He wants you to have life and have it more abundantly. By denying yourself, hopefully you will come to a place where you finally admit that nothing you do physically or mentally is capable of removing your sin, whipping your demons, or setting you free from sin habits that keep you from learning to live for God!

You must accept that you cannot do it! Deny yourself. Jesus was talking about placing your faith in what He did for you on the Cross, only on the Cross, and trusting God's GRACE towards you, His goodness towards you on a daily basis. God's GRACE is not a Christian cliché. His Cross is the access to His power. His Cross now becomes YOUR Cross, because you are in Christ. He did it for you! Recognize that biblical fact. This is how you take up your Cross daily.

For too many years, the church has erroneously taught men and women, who desperately want to live for God but have found themselves failing miserably so that their only option seems to be to **do more** and **work harder** at what does not work permanently. This erroneous teaching continues the cycle of encouraging well-meaning and well-intentioned Believers to revert back to what they know best, working harder!

The Cross was the instrument of Christ's death and remains the symbol of His death. This death must be a mortal blow to our ego, to our belief in our own abilities, no matter how successful we think we are in life or in a ministry. It is the death of our own self-reliance. It is complete and total trust in what Jesus did on that Cross for us. This must be a daily realization in our lives in spirit and in truth!

Straying from this bible truth, by necessity, means you will revert back to yourself! Although you may experience varying degrees of "success", **self is the essential ingredient to the sin of pride.**

Pride goes before a fall
Proverbs 16:16

Chapter 7

All of Him, NONE of Me!

The most resistance I have personally experienced to the message of God's GRACE comes from other Believers. For whatever reason, generally, because of what they have been taught, Believers think that the message of God's GRACE, God's rest, and learning the ability to trust Him for every aspect of their lives just doesn't sit well at first.

The power of God's GRACE, and the message of God's GRACE, available to every Believer, goes against our old sin nature and what we have been taught as Believers. As Pastor Joseph Prince says often, "The message of God's GRACE is nothing new. It is the message of the Gospel. It is the message that Paul preached." *www.Josephprince.com* He is correct!

Getting people to realize that their works, their actions, and their Christian disciplines will never substitute for the work of the Holy Spirit in their lives is not an easy task. Bible reading, prayer, fasting, memorizing Scripture, taking the Lord's Supper are all good Christian disciplines. They must not be ignored! However, if you are counting on these, you will never have complete victory over the wiles of the devil which seeks your destruction! You will never have a full appreciation for the goodness of God, and that lack of understanding, or lack of appreciation, will keep you from receiving the many wondrous blessings God has in store for you!

Most Bible teachers teach the definition of GRACE to be unmerited or unearned favor. That is correct. However, I prefer to look at the GRACE of God as the goodness of God. His GRACE or His goodness towards us cannot be contained. It is a never ending supply. So when I speak of the GRACE of God, I am speaking of God's goodness. They are one in the same!

The Whole Armor of God?

Children's Sunday schools teach about the "armor of God" found in Ephesians 6. Paul uses the language so that anyone familiar with Rome would identify with it. I believe many are teaching these verses about the *armor* in such a way that they are creating a false sense of security in something God never intended to be doctrinal! Remember, Ephesians 6:10 says, "Finally, my brethren, be strong **in the Lord** and the **power of his might."** This is God's armor, not yours! In Ephesians 6, Paul never taught us to "visualize" or pretend we are putting this armor on! "Visualization" is a common technique used by New Age Religions and should not be a part of a true Believer's daily devotion or life. We only wear this armor as we are in Christ and He is in us. The Holy Spirit through the apostle Paul was demonstrating just how comprehensive Christ's victory on the Cross was for us. Paul used the same language in Romans 13:14 when he said, "... Put on the Lord Jesus Christ..."

Put on the whole armor of God that you may be able to stand against the wiles of the devil.
Ephesians 6:11

Standing against the wiles of the devil will come effortlessly as you remain in Christ!

For we do not wrestle against flesh and blood, but against principalities, against powers, against the rulers of the darkness of this age, against spiritual hosts of wickedness in the heavenly places. Therefore take up the whole armor of God, that you may be able to withstand in the evil day, and having done all, to stand. Stand therefore, having girded your waist with truth, having put on the breastplate of righteousness, and having shod your feet with the preparation of the gospel of peace, above all, taking the shield of faith with which you will be able to quench all the fiery darts of the wicked one. And take the helmet of

salvation, and the sword of the Spirit, which is the word of God.
Ephesians 6:12-17

*...***the breastplate of righteousness***...* There is only one who is righteous. That is Jesus.
1 John 2:1

*...***having shod your feet with the preparation of the gospel of peace***...* There is nothing about the gospel of peace that does not involve Jesus!

*"...above all, taking the **shield of faith**..."*

Faith in what? If we have to rely on how strong we think our faith is, we are in serious trouble. This is why so many of our Christian brothers and sisters are falling around us. The faith referred to here is faith in the death, burial, and resurrection of your Lord and Savior, Jesus Christ. He provided His goodness. He provided the finished work on the Cross so that you and I need only to place our faith in one thing, His goodness for us, His GRACE for us, and the finished work He did at the Cross!

When we get hit with those fiery darts, and we will get hit with them from time to time, it is only because of what Jesus did at the Cross that those fiery darts can be quenched. This is God's GRACE toward you, and although it might hurt your feelings, you had nothing to do with that work! As you trust Him, and what

He did for you, you realize the Lord's GRACE and His goodness toward you knows no bounds.

"...And take the helmet of salvation..."

None of these teachings, none of these victories, are available to those who have not been born-again. If you have not experienced true salvation in Christ, none of these writings are going to help you.

But without faith it is impossible to please Him, for he who comes to God must believe that He is, and that He is a rewarder of those who diligently seek Him.
Hebrews 11:6

In the beginning was the Word, and the Word was with God and the Word was God. Jesus is God! Our armor is not of this world. It protects us only in proportion to our faith and dependence on what Jesus did for us at the Cross! It certainly does not depend upon our self-efforts or our good works. It is there (in the spirit world) for our protection BECAUSE we are in Christ.

If you are a Bible scholar to any degree, you may correctly point out that the "word" referred to in Ephesians 6:17 in the Greek, is the word "rema", not "logos" as it is in John 1:1. My point is this. **All** Scripture (all *graphe* in the greek) directly or indirectly points to

Jesus Christ and his purpose for coming to earth. **John 5:39**

When you "put on" Jesus Christ as described in **Romans 13:14** and other scriptures, <u>you are "putting on" the armor of God!</u>

To place your faith in anything other than the Cross of Christ, which provides God's GRACE and God's goodness for you, is to veer off God's plan to get closer to Him. Your victory over sin, the flesh, and your temptations comes by GRACE and the victory won by Jesus on the Cross FOR you. **His victory is now your victory.** His protection is now your protection. His armor is now your armor. How silly some of us must have looked pretending to put this armor on just because we were taught to do so.

And I, brethren, if I still preach circumcision, why do I still suffer persecution? Then the offense of the Cross has ceased.
Galatians 5:11

The apostle Paul spent the majority of his time teaching and writing in the New Testament just how wrong the Judaizers were. Sadly, we have many today who claim to be Christians, but they are no different than the Judaizers of old. Believers, who claim that you are saved by GRACE, but that you must keep the Law (or certain Old Testament Laws), are no different today. They say, like the Judaizers of old, that you are saved by GRACE but... *You must be circumcised,... You must observe the Sabbath, ... You must keep the feast days.* The list of the demands Judaizers place on true Believers goes on and on. This mixture of GRACE and works and GRACE and Law, is the exact reason why the apostle Paul argued with the apostle Peter to his face! Peter later came around and agreed with Paul.

> *But when I saw that they were not straightforward about the truth of the gospel, I said to Peter before them all, "If you, being a Jew, live in the manner of Gentiles and not as the Jews, why do you[b] compel Gentiles to live as Jews? We who are Jews by nature, and not sinners of the Gentiles, knowing that a man is not justified by the works of the law but by faith in Jesus Christ, even we have believed in Christ Jesus, that we might be justified by faith in Christ and not by the works of the law, for by the works of the law no flesh shall be justified.*
> **Galatians 2:14-16**

It is through faith alone in Christ alone and by GRACE and GRACE alone that you were saved. That same GRACE that saved you is the same GRACE that keeps you! The reason why you are not drawing closer to God or seeing victories in your life as a Christian is because you are not asking!!! Twelve step programs, self-help books, your own willpower; these things will ONLY result in temporary victory, a few weeks or months at best. **STOP TRYING AND START ASKING!**

Just like Dorothy in the Wizard of Oz, **the answer** to your problem, the answer to your victory, **is right at your feet**. Or more accurately said, right at the foot of the Cross! If you want to live for God, you are only going to do so by exercising your faith in what Jesus did for you personally and do it daily! When you make your addiction(s) or your trouble(s), God's problem, HE, and HE alone, gives you 100% permanent success. SIMPLY ASK and keep asking! This way, God gets the Glory, YOU get the victory!

Chapter 8

Victory in Jesus!

For I determined not to know anything among you except Jesus Christ and Him crucified.
1 Corinthians 2:2

If you have been involved in Christianity for any length of time, you no doubt have heard or participated in churches or groups or saw national speakers calling for revival, a return to God in our country. God is pouring His Spirit over and through every Believer who asks and pouring it abundantly! We are in the great revival that we have been seeking! For many years, we have been looking upward or outward for this revival when all along God has been doing marvelous works in us on the inside. All we have to do is receive it.

Thousands of pastors today are still handing out the same erroneous advice to Christians worldwide regardless of what the problem is. Read the Bible more, pray more, go to church more, take communion more often, or work harder, none of which will bring you permanently closer to God. God's biblical plan is that the Cross of Christ and God's GRACE takes center stage in your life daily or even hourly.

What would you tell someone who is struggling to overcome a reoccurring sin in their life like anger, rage, lust, homosexuality, or drug addiction?

Just read your Bible more?

Memorize a certain amount of Scriptures?

Have more faith?

Go see a psychologist or psychiatrist?

Just pray more?

Go to a Christian Twelve Step Program?

Get a confidential buddy?

As Christians, we do not get the option of shaping and molding God's methods of bringing us closer to Himself, of giving us victory over our sins. The only factor that is common between Jesus and twelve step programs is the number twelve, twelve disciples, twelve steps. Even that was done as a reflection of the twelve tribes of Israel. It had nothing to do with any "magic" number or other prescribed method by God to bring you closer to Him.

Every one of these "works" are self-efforts; you trying to accomplish overcoming your problems through your own intellect or your own efforts or obeying guidelines or rules. Remember, God is a jealous God. HE will not share His victory with anyone, not even you! In our sincere desire to draw closer to the Lord, many of us have been down one or more of these dead end paths. Many will tell you they prayed on their knees or on their faces, seeking to draw closer to God and freedom from their reoccurring sins. Others will tell you they memorized Scripture until their eyes got tired. The list of "weapons" we use is very long. When these methods do not bring about the desired or expected results, thousands upon thousands walk away due to frustration, anger, or a failed faith.

"...Behold, a sower went out to sow. And as he sowed, some seed fell by the wayside, and the birds came and devoured them. Some fell on stony places, where they did not have much earth, and they immediately sprang up because they had no depth of earth. But when the sun was up they were scorched, and because they had no root they withered away. And some fell among thorns, and the thorns sprang up and choked them... He who has ears to hear, let him hear!"
Matthew 13:3-9

If devoting a certain amount of hours participating in a particular discipline was the answer, how many hours is it? This same question can be asked of any man-made answer to your sin problem or in your desire to draw closer to God. In those cases, your attempts work against your victory and your sanctification. We often get confused and think by doing X, Y, or Z long enough or sincerely enough, eventually God will give us the breakthrough we are seeking. God's way is the only way.

Biblical disciplines, in and of themselves, are not bad for you. In fact, they are required of every Believer. However, these disciplines, if they are to help you draw closer to God at all, must be *post facto* to the Cross and the acceptance of the price Jesus paid. Otherwise, it is exactly like placing the proverbial cart before the horse.

Remember, holiness is not the way to Christ. Christ is the way to holiness. Your Christian disciplines must flow from your relationship with Jesus and what he did for you on the Cross. That is the power of His resurrection. We must let our light shine, but it also must start at the Cross and God's GRACE and not with anything in our flesh. You cannot accomplish anything godly on the inside of you by anything you do or don't do on the outside. It is a work of the Holy Spirit!

When I finally grasped this simple yet crucial truth, it revolutionized my walk with the Lord. When I get out of the way of His GRACE towards me and my sanctification, it is then that Christ can continued His work in me. I truly am in Christ, and I truly am a new creature. Old things are passed away and behold all things are still becoming new. He is the vine, we are the branches. **Without Him, we can do nothing. John 15:5**

This should not be a unique experience to most Believers. But sadly, it has become so. My spiritual walk, my praying without ceasing, has only been in direct proportion to my kneeling at the foot of the Cross and accepting God's GRACE, God's goodness towards me on a daily basis. It is not my self-effort, but God working IN me.

Chapter 9

Producing Fruit!

Even so, every good tree bears good fruit, but a bad tree bears bad fruit.
Matthew 7:17

During my childhood years, I spent many of my summers living with my Italian grandmother in Atlantic City, the area commonly known as Little Italy. Just west of the convention hall in Atlantic City is Florida Avenue. Although no longer there, running perpendicular to Florida Avenue north and south was Florida Terrace. It was an area of two rows of brick and mortar buildings, two and three story high houses occupied by Italian immigrants and their descendants. As a young boy, I would follow my grandmother to the market. She would spend an extraordinary amount of time picking up pieces of various fruits and vegetables and examining each one, either putting it back or putting it in her basket. I could never understand how my grandmother could stand there examining the fruit for what seemed like hours. Yet, if my friends and I walked near the market without our parents or grandparents, we would hear the owner yell, "**NO- TOUCHA- DA- FRUIT**!!!!!" My friends and I would run and scurry in various directions.

In our hurried and rushed lives today, it is still not uncommon for women to examine the produce in the fruit and vegetable aisles. This is what we love about the teachings of Jesus. Although he was teaching us life long, kingdom principles, he used examples applicable in everyday lives. Just about everybody can identify with examining fruit.

How many good trees bear good fruit? The answer is, of course, ALL good trees bear good fruit. What does this actually mean? What was Jesus trying to get a Cross to us? To begin with, let me clear up one misconception about good and bad fruit. Jesus was not talking about two very different looking trees. In fact, the trees that He is teaching us about look very similar. It is the fruit that He instructed us to produce and examine. This is why when He said in the 16th verse of Matthew 7, "*Do men gather grapes from thorn-bushes or figs from thistles?*" He was showing us that these fruits look the same, but yet, some are good and some are bad. Nobody goes to a thorn bush and expects to pick apples!

The deeper teaching here is that the fruits look the same. Two apples next to each other look the same and they may smell the same. Yet, one may have good fruit inside and the other is corrupted. It is entirely possible for a man or a woman inside of church to look like a "Christian". A person, by their very nature, may be a very moderate, temperate person. They may simply have learned good manners and to be considerate of others. That is not the Holy Spirit change that Jesus was teaching. It is the regenerative work of the Holy Spirit making changes on the inside that makes a person produce good "fruit".

What is taking place on the inside of a person that qualifies him or her as a good or bad "fruit?" As we continue to read in **Matthew Chapter 7,** Jesus continues to talk about those who come to Him espousing all the wonderful things they did in His name. He rebukes them by saying, "I never knew you!" Later on in **Matthew Chapter 12,** Jesus continues this theme when speaking of the evilness of the religious leaders of the day. He called them "*Vipers!"*

How can you, being evil, speak good things? For out of the abundance of the heart the mouth speaks. A good man out of the good treasure of his heart brings forth good things, and an evil man out of the evil treasure brings forth evil things".
Matthew 12: 34-35

This teaching by Jesus is somewhat complicated in that just prior to teaching about these fruits of the Spirit, he exhorts us not to judge one another. So what is the distinction? Well, the easy answer on the surface is that we judge the person's fruit or actions, and not the actual person. So how do we separate the person's fruits from the actual person themselves?

Let's go back to the two fruit trees or the two apples that look alike. One is a good fruit and the other is a bad fruit. It's not until we bite into the fruit that we know the difference. It is not until a person reveals what is on the inside of them that we are able to judge whether their fruit is good or not. Fortunately for us, the methods or standards that we are to judge the fruits by are listed in the Bible!

*But the **fruit** of the Spirit is love, joy, peace, longsuffering, kindness, goodness, faithfulness, gentleness, self-control. Against such there is no law. And those who are Christ's have crucified the flesh with its passions and desires. If we live in the Spirit, let us also walk in the Spirit. Let us not become conceited, provoking one another, envying one another.*
Galatians 5:22-26

Finally, brethren, whatever things are true, whatever things are noble, whatever things are just, whatever things are pure, whatever things are lovely, whatever things are of good

report, if there is any virtue and if there is anything praiseworthy—meditate on these things. The things which you learned and received and heard and saw in me, these do, and the God of peace will be with you.
Philippians 4:8-9

Anybody can play church!

As the late Pastor Adrian Rogers once said, "There are a lot of big babies in churches today who are saved, but they are immature. You can only be young once, but you can be immature as a Believer for a lifetime. You can be born-again and then just stop growing. In most churches today, there are far too many people who are babies when they should be Giants!"

He went on further to say, "There are three types of people in churches today - natural, spiritual, and carnal. With the natural man, spiritual growth is impossible. You can take an old dead stick, place it in the ground, water it, feed it, give it sunlight, and it will still never grow! The natural person has no spiritual life."

But the natural man does not receive the things of the Spirit of God, for they are foolishness to him, nor can he know them, because they are spiritually discerned.
1 Corinthians 2:14

A natural person can appreciate the things in church like the sound of the choir, the comfort of the seats, the friendliness of the people and other external factors. But, they will not understand the gospel message. It is like taking a dog to the opera.

A carnal person is saved, but displays little if any spiritual growth. They have retarded development and spiritual growth is impaired.

And I, brethren, could not speak to you as to spiritual people but as to carnal, as to babes in Christ. I fed you with milk and not with solid food, for until now you were not able to receive it, and even now you are still not able
1 Corinthians 3:1-2

When children are first born and as they are growing up, they do and say the cutest things. They say, "daa-daa" and "ma-ma". However, there is something very wrong with staying a baby. When my three daughters were growing up, they were the cutest kids in the world. I'm sure yours were as well. But, if one of my grown daughters had started talking or acting like an infant, something would have been very wrong! We are all expected to grow as Christians! We are all expected to learn.

Where we go wrong is thinking that reading the latest book or practicing the latest fad will somehow help us learn to live for God. Nothing takes the place of a relationship and allowing

God, Himself, to teach us through His Word, mold us and allow Him to make us grow.

If you are a baby, you have to eat baby food like strained beets, carrots and milk! Sadly, for some, all the spiritual food some people get is what they get in church once a week. Their pastor becomes their spiritual nursemaid who bottle feeds them and burps them on the way out of the door on Sunday mornings. If you are a new Believer, you need to be fed and nurtured, but eventually you have to start eating solid food which is the Word!

As newborn babes, desire the pure milk of the word, that you may grow thereby.
1 Peter 2:2

The idea is that, sooner or later, you start feeding yourself so that you can begin to feed others.

For though by this time you ought to be teachers, you need someone to teach you again the first principles of the oracles of God, and you have come to need milk and not solid food.
Hebrews 5:12

Subsequently, throughout the entire New Testament, we have been given rulers, yardsticks, and measuring devices to judge whether a "fruit" is good or bad. Mature

Believers will make a conscientious decision to separate their opinions about a person's fruit from the actual person themselves. In fact, if someone you know claims to be a Christian, and does not produce good fruit, there is a very good chance he or she may not be saved.

It is possible to have an intellectual grasp and understanding of Christianity without a relationship with Jesus. This is what makes them LOOK like Christians on the outside. It is possible for a person to be intelligent enough to say all the right things at all the right times. But, if this person does not have the regenerative work of the Holy Spirit in their lives, eventually their fruit will show itself to be corrupt.

People like this will show narcissistic tendencies, although they may seem to care about others. The truth of the matter is that their interactions with others are nothing but a means to gain an end for themselves. They may want sympathy or money. They may want a position in church or authority over others. There may be many other self-serving purposes for their friendship with you.

Regardless of their motives, these "Christians" are all about themselves and not about the Lord. They are people that start almost every conversation talking about themselves. If they mention you at all it is only as a segue to begin talking about themselves. That is very corrupt fruit and they may not even be Christians at all. True Christianity is to be lived by a person from the inside out, not a façade or merely intellectually displayed.

Carnal Christians, those who are walking in their flesh, will become more evident and more apparent to you as you interact with them. Don't criticize them! Don't judge them! Don't try and teach them what you are learning in any other way but through patience and love. Understand, many of your Christian friends and relatives may never catch on to God's GRACE and its availability to their lives. If you have, treasure it. Thank Him for it, but never become critical of those around you who have not learned. Thank the Lord that you have learned and pray for those Believers who have not.

> *These are sensual persons, who cause divisions, not having the Spirit.*
> **Jude 1:19**

Carnal Christians are the ones who cause divisions in churches by insisting on having things their way. They do not have a spirit of patience and love. Most Pastors have more problems with carnal Christians, and their silly bickering and complaining, than they do with drugs and drug addicts. Often times, carnal Christians are able to quote Scripture better than most of us. They can find a theological argument in a jot or a tittle. These grumblers will get upset over the dumbest things if they do not get their way, especially in church!

They concern themselves with things like which side of the church the flag should be on, why isn't the parking lot lit up better, the doors in the church squeak too much, the music is too loud, the music is too soft, it is too cold in here, or it is too hot in here. *Fill in your own petty example here!*

Carnal Christians cause squabbles expecting their pastor to go around the church and put pacifiers in everybody's mouth. They need to grow up!

Why am I belaboring this point? Because, **carnal Christians do not have the GRACE of God and the goodness of God at the core of their daily lives.** They do not appreciate the Cross of Jesus Christ and what He did for them personally. If they did, they would never act as foolish as they sometimes do. Unless otherwise directed by the Lord, it may be best to leave these people out of your social circles and seek others who are like minded.

But you are not in the flesh but in the Spirit, if indeed the Spirit of God dwells in you. Now if anyone does not have the Spirit of Christ, he is not His.
Romans 8:9

And those who are Christ's have crucified the flesh with its passions and desires.
Galatians 5:24

It is important not to characterize or judge any individual as a good or bad person based on the type of fruit they produce. We are all at different levels of learning in the Lord! Just because I see a man who claims to be a Christian smoking a cigarette does not mean he is a bad person or a bad piece of fruit. He may be a new Believer whom the Lord is shaping and molding. The Lord, Himself, may be working on other areas in this man's life making the cigarette smoking the least of his transgressions at this time in his life.

Now, on the other hand, if this same man comes into church and starts teaching that every Christian should smoke cigarettes; that would be really bad fruit!

D. Martyn Lloyd-Jones writes, "*...a man who has washed on the surface only may give all appearance of being a Christian. But our Lord's argument is that what really decides whether he is one or not is the nature within. And that nature within is bound to express itself.... We can say, therefore, that true Christian belief must of a necessity produce that characteristic type of living... A man's true inward belief is bound to manifest itself, sooner or later, in his life. We must be careful therefore, that we do not mistake for the real thing that which looks*

like true Christianity, but which is in reality
merely sham and only outward appearance."
(Studies in the Sermon on the Mount, D. Martyn Lloyd-Jones.
Copyright 1959).

Churches are overloaded with people who act
one way in church and act completely
differently at home or outside church. Jesus
had a name for these types of people:
hypocrites! They become Satan's first line of
attack to keep people away from church!

How do I produce good fruit or how can I know
that the fruit I'm producing is good? I am so
glad you asked! All of the attributes of a true
Christian Believer listed in Philippians and
Galatians and throughout the New Testament,
are not a checklist of characteristics that must
be displayed or goals to be reached. One
should never look at these verses and say to
themselves, "I'm not gentle, therefore, I need
to find the latest *how-to book* on how to
become gentle." Nor should any Christian say
to themselves, "I'm not at peace, therefore, I
need to meet with someone so that I may
learn to have peace."

The evidence, the fruit of the spirit, spoken of
throughout the Bible is never the work of man
or a result of man's efforts to produce these
fruits. The work of the Holy Spirit in a person's
life is just that; it is a work of the Spirit, not
the person! No tree planted in the middle of
the garden stands there and exerts
tremendous effort, squeezing each twig and

branch, working hard to produce fruit. It is a natural process orchestrated and ordained by God.

As people surrender more and more of themselves, the free flow of the Holy Spirit allows the Holy Spirit to produce the fruit. Sometimes the simplest answers are the hardest ones to process.

YOU MUST ASK!

"So I say to you, ask, and it will be given to you, seek; and you will find; knock, and it will be opened to you. For everyone who asks receives, and he who seeks finds, and to him who knocks it will be opened. If a son asks for bread[d] from any father among you, will he give him a stone? Or if he asks for a fish, will he give him a serpent instead of a fish? Or if he asks for an egg, will he offer him a scorpion? If you then, being evil, know how to give good gifts to your children, how much more will your heavenly Father give the Holy Spirit to those who ask Him!"
Luke 11:9-13

Chapter 10

Married to Jesus!

If you ask your boss for a raise, and he or she is willing to grant you that raise on one condition, the condition being that you must clean up your desk every Friday before you go home from work. You may say, "That's no problem. I can clean up my desk in under one minute, so yes, we have a deal. I'll take the raise." Others may say, "That's unreasonable. I deserve this raise. I earned this raise, and I refuse to allow my boss to attach strings to what I deserve!"

So goes the work of sanctification in your life as a Believer. God's goodness and His GRACE towards you knows no bounds. He literally only asks one thing, broken in two parts, in return. 1. Be willing to surrender more of yourself as He works in your life.

2. Sustained communication (prayer) with Him on a daily basis that never ceases.

I heard the late Pastor Adrian Rogers say once, "Many of us treat God like the recently married bride. Joe and Mary are in the car having just been married and are on their way to their honeymoon. Mary looks at Joe and says, 'Oh Joe, this is the best day of my life! The wedding was perfect. Our dresses looked perfect. You and the groomsmen were dressed perfectly. The reception was perfect, and it was everything I had dreamed of since I was a little girl. NOW TAKE ME HOME TO MY MOTHER!' 'What?' Joe blurts out. 'Yes', Mary says. 'We are going to stay married and see each other on the holidays. If I need anything, I'll be sure to call you first, but take me home to my mother!'"

This is the way too many of us treat God. You can be married to someone for a very long time. You get along just fine, and you rarely, if ever, fight and argue. But, if there is not that daily communication, intimacy of relationship, sharing and caring, you do not have a marriage. You have a business arrangement! God is not looking for a business arrangement with you. He is looking to become intricately involved in every aspect of your life. Why? Because He wants to control your every move and every thought? God forbid, NO! He knows what is best for you. He knows what is right for you. Only He can guide your life in such a way that you will avoid many of life's pitfalls and snares so that only He can bless you as He always intended.

God's blessings on you will be in direct proportion to your willingness to surrender more of your life and to kneel at the foot of the Cross realizing the price that He paid for this privilege. You must place all of your faith in what Jesus did for you at the Cross. It is sufficient for all eternity in our lives. It is more than sufficient to overcome temptation in your life. Too many of us have drifted away from the simplicity and unspeakable magnitude of the Cross of Christ. As long as the Cross of Jesus Christ stays between your heart and your sin, you will stay protected! Being willing to surrender more of yourself to the Lord and staying in communication with Him daily or even hourly gives the Holy Spirit the latitude to work on the inside of you producing good fruit.

For you did not receive the spirit of bondage again to fear, but you received the Spirit of adoption by whom we cry out, "Abba, Father."
Romans 8:15

When we were new Christians, the excitement of our new birth was exhilarating, but somewhere along the way many of us lose our joy. Yet, we train ourselves to put on a happy face at church. We somehow think that we are messed up and everybody else has it all figured out. So, we act within certain parameters when we get around other Christians, especially in church. Instead of addressing the core of the problems we are facing, we simply fall into the same traps we and others have created as potential answers to those problems. These traps are designed by the enemy to keep us as far away from the goodness of God, His GRACE, and the Cross, as much as possible.

And the apostles said to the Lord, "Increase our faith."
Luke 17:5

Remember, holiness is not the way to God. Christ is the way to holiness. You're Christian disciplines must flow FROM your relationship with Jesus, your understanding by faith of what He did for you at the Cross, and the power of His resurrection. You cannot accomplish anything on the inside by anything you do or don't do on the outside. It is a work of the Holy Spirit and must remain so!

So without understanding it, many of us have fallen into the failed cycle of works and the Law when the actual answer to getting close to God is **asking and surrendering.**

Without understanding God's GRACE towards you, without Jesus being the center of your faith, your daily life and walk will drift away from Him.

For I determined not to know anything among you except Jesus Christ and Him crucified.
1 Corinthians 2:2

You must receive the GRACE of God, and understanding that His GRACE and His goodness towards you did not end when you first got saved. In fact, that is when it just got started. Recognizing the need for God's GRACE daily keeps you growing in the Lord. This will help you understand the blessings you continue to receive from Him, all because of his GRACE.

Everything God gives the Believer in this dispensation of GRACE is done only through His love for us, received by faith. His GRACE is sufficient for your sanctification, as well as your salvation. When we follow Jesus in the light of His sacrifice on the Cross, we are following Him in spirit and in deed. This brings the Believer closer to God! HE NEVER FAILS US!

So, am I saying that ordinances of the church, such as communion and fasting, are works of the flesh? No, I am not saying that. What I am saying is that they can be!

Let's start with Communion.

I think it's safe to say we all agree that Communion is a New Testament ordinance of the church instituted by Jesus. Most Bible believing churches often serve communion in accordance with the words of Jesus.

*And He took bread, gave thanks and broke it,
and gave it to them, saying, "This is My body
which is given for you; do this in remembrance
of Me." Likewise He also took the cup after
supper, saying, "This cup is the new covenant
in My blood, which is shed for you.*
Luke 22:19-20

Communion is actually a biblical ordinance of
the church tracing its roots all the way back to
the first High Priest, Melchizedek. **Genesis
14:18**

How often a particular church participates in
communion is entirely up to the individual
church. However, I think many pastors teach
incorrectly that Christians must examine
themselves before they participate in taking
communion. They will teach that, prior to
taking Communion, one must examine oneself
to see if there is any unconfessed sins in his or
her life or not. This is out of context! Let's look
at the verse that many pastors will use to
teach this incorrectly.

*Therefore whoever eats this bread or drinks
this cup of the Lord in an unworthy manner will
be guilty of the body and blood of the Lord.
But let a man examine himself, and so let him
eat of the bread and drink of the cup. For he
who eats and drinks in an unworthy manner
eats and drinks judgment to himself, not
discerning the Lord's body. For this reason
many are weak and sick among you, and many*

sleep. For if we would judge ourselves, we would not be judged.
1 Corinthians 11:26-31

Many of us have been taught that before we can take communion, we need to contemplate whether we are in right standing with the Lord, and if there are unconfessed sins in our lives, we must make them right before we partake! Otherwise, we may get sick or die prematurely. After all, this is what the Bible says, right? How does that correspond with the message of GRACE? If the Cross was a finished work (and it was), how does this "examination" fit in?

Truthfully, as taught by many, it doesn't. When you accepted Christ for the forgiveness of your sins, ALL of your sins were forgiven. They were thrown as far as the east is to the west. Remember, I told you earlier that context is king with a small "k".

The context of Paul's teaching in this regard is communion being served in the church of Corinth whose people were involved in riotous living and gluttony. They began to erroneously call their daily meals communion or used communion as a substitute for daily meals. Paul was very much correcting these acts of their flesh and their cavalier attitude towards Holy Communion. They were trying to accomplish taking communion and eating dinner, in essence, trying to kill two birds with one stone.

That was the first part of the Apostle Paul trying to set the record straight. The second part revolves around the "examining" of oneself. What Paul was asking them to consider, what he was asking them to "examine", was whether or not they were in the Faith. In other words, what are you trusting for your eternal salvation? Are you trusting the fact that you are eating a wafer of bread and drinking from a cup of grape juice every week or every month because it's a good thing to do? Or, are you truly in the Faith, trusting what Jesus said and did for you over 2000 years ago? Examine if you are partaking of Holy Communion because you identify with Jesus as one of his disciples, or are you merely participating in communion because it seems right and looks like a good thing to do? There is a distinct and life-changing difference!

This brings me to the ordinance of Fasting.

Fasting, too, is a biblical ordinance of the church going all the way back to the time of Nehemiah. **Nehemiah 9:1**

The dictionary defines fasting as *abstaining from all food, to eat only sparingly or of certain kinds of food, especially as a religious observance.* dictionary.reference.com

Recently, Christians have "fasted" things like television, movies, golf or recreational fun. The

Bible does not directly reference fasting in any other context but food. However, having said that, the Bible does not forbid fasting such things either.

Over the years, many Christian churches have taken the ordinance of fasting out of context. They will teach it as the latest fad or as God's special diet plan! This borders on blasphemy. The ordinance of fasting to a Believer should be motivated by a deeper desire to live for God or a desire to draw closer to Him! Let's examine the true, deeper meaning of why a Believer should fast.

The idea of fasting is to disrupt the daily routine of Believers in such a way that they are prompted to commune with God or pray to God at times of the day or night that they may not normally do so. This prompting is caused by a small degree of physical discomfort. You are fasting. You get hungry, and normally, you would grab a snack or prepare a meal and satisfy your hunger. When fasting, rather than satisfying your flesh, you are reminded to pray. There are no set rules or regulations for fasting before the Lord. A believer may fast a meal, a day, or, in some cases, as long as a week. Jesus fasted for 40 days and 40 nights, but he was God. You are not! **Matthew 4:2**

(Author's note: At no time should anyone fast his or her medications or water. Nothing in the Bible suggests that any Christian should jeopardize their health or well-being for the sake of fasting.)

However, the most important teaching that Jesus gave regarding a fast has been severely diluted over the years. Recently, churches have begun to teach fasting as a way to prompt God to respond in a particular form or fashion. Fasting to try and get God to answer a specific prayer, or prayers, runs contrary to the Gospel of GRACE. Remember, Jesus said;

...I have come that they may have life, and that they may have it more abundantly.
John 10:10(b)

Nowhere in the Bible did Jesus ever prequalify His desire to answer your prayers on the condition that you fast!

The deeper truth about fasting that I think has been lost over the years is that of secrecy and intimacy with the Lord. Let's use the words of Jesus, Himself, to explain:

*Moreover, when you fast, **do not be like the hypocrites**, with a sad countenance. For they disfigure their faces that they may appear to men to be fasting. Assuredly, I say to you, **they have their reward**. But you, when you fast, anoint your head and wash your face, so that you do not appear to men to be fasting, but to your Father who is in the secret place;*

and your Father who sees in secret will reward you openly.
Matthew 6:16-18

I am trying to teach you throughout this entire book, your personal relationship with the Lord should be ongoing - hourly or (at least) daily in your life! **Give us this day** our daily bread. You cannot store up enough "Jesus" to get through the week. If your relationship with the Lord consists only of going to church once a week, this book probably will not help you! In order to live for God and receive His blessings constantly and continually, you must stay in communion with Him through prayer often.

Earlier in Chapter 6 in the book of Matthew Jesus spoke about giving "alms" or money to the church. Tithing or giving your local church ten percent of your weekly income is a biblical ordinance as well, but this will remain a subject for another book. It is sufficient to say that the biblical equivalent of a "storehouse" is your local church. If your church is actively doing the will of God by seeking to save the lost, they deserve your financial support! The Lord only requires ten percent; the Government takes much more than that!
Malachi 3:10

Again, if you are not careful, the giving of alms and fasting can result in a work of your flesh if your motives for doing so are self-serving. In keeping with the context of Matthew Chapter

6, Jesus said, "Wh*en you do these things to be seen of others, you have already received your reward!"* It is not uncommon in churches today to hear well-meaning Christians brag about their giving or their fasting. By doing so, according to Jesus, they forfeit their heavenly reward in return for an earthly one.

When fasting for the Lord, this should remain an intimate secret between you and God. It is a physical way of surrendering more of your flesh, your valuable time, your entertainment, to God in return for a closer walk with Him.

I will be honest with you, I cannot remember the last time I fasted. It is not because I do not believe it is biblical. It is. But, as I tell our Congregation in Arizona, I feel closer to Jesus today than I did yesterday. I simply have not felt compelled to fast since learning of God's goodness and his GRACE towards me. I did, however, feel compelled to write this book, hoping and praying you will learn the joy of walking with the Lord every day as I have. This may be a topic for another study, but I am living the life that Jesus described in **Matthew 9:14-15**

Draw near to God and He will draw near to you...
James 4:8(a)

I need to caution you at this point. Maybe an imaginary lightbulb has gone off in your head regarding God's GRACE towards you and your sanctification. It does seem almost too easy. Then why do people struggle with these biblical truths? There are many reasons, mostly because of a lack of sound biblical teaching in the church.

My people are destroyed for lack of knowledge. Because you have rejected knowledge,...
Hosea 4:6

Additionally, retooling our brains from a mentality of "works and performance" to relying on God's GRACE by faith and what Jesus did for you on the Cross sounds easy, but it takes time. It is a bit like an infant letting go of the couch or the chair in order to walk for the first time.

Taking comfort in your good works or your performances as a way of pleasing God, and subsequently expecting good in return, is applying only the MILK of the Word and not the MEAT!

I fed you with milk and not with solid food, for until now you were not able to receive it, and even now you are still not able, for you are still carnal (in your flesh). For where there are envy, strife, and divisions among you, are you not carnal and behaving like mere men?
1 Corinthians 3:2-3

No, my friend, if you have a sincere heart to draw closer to God, it is not going to be done by keeping the Law through your good works or your efforts. Drawing closer to God is a work of God's GRACE in your life accepted by faith as you surrender more of yourself to the Lord every day. It is liberating!

For though by this time you ought to be teachers, you need someone to teach you again the first principles of the oracles of God, and you have come to need milk and not solid food. For everyone who partakes only of milk is unskilled in the word of righteousness, for he is a babe. But solid food belongs to those who are of full age, that is, those who by reason of use have their senses exercised to discern both good and evil.
Hebrews 5:12-14

Chapter 11

Do Good, Get Good, Do Bad, Get...

Far too many pastors are teaching their flocks cause and effect. If I caused the hammer to fall, the hammer will hit the ground. If I just obey my mother and father, I get the candy that I want. As long as I'm nice to that person, we will get along just fine. Our entire lives are integrated with the teaching that if we do good, we should get good and if we do bad, we deserve bad. This is not the way it works with God! None of us deserves His goodness, yet it is poured out by God on every Believer who is willing to receive.

When people first get saved, it is only natural to want to do good works. I keep going back to that new Believer who ended his testimony at our church by saying, "I am going to spend the rest of my life paying Him back for what He did for me." THAT is a very natural and normal reaction to the miracle of the new birth. But the truth is we can never repay the Lord for what He has done. He wants a relationship with you, not your good works.

But go and learn what this means: I desire mercy and not sacrifice: for I did not come to call the righteous, but sinners, to repentance.
Matthew 9:13(a)

By doing good "works", whatever they are to you, you gain a degree of comfort in your new birth. You then, bring much of doing good "works" (worldly ways) into the church. It is our nature to work for rewards. We meet other Christians in church who bring their good "works" in with them as well. Although their "works" may not have been the same as yours, you were both doing "good" for the Lord. Nobody ever questions their motives in church, and they certainly never questioned mine. No one ever taught us differently!

The problem is that these new man-made laws/works we create to help us get closer to God do not work against sin. They will work only to the extent that we trust what Christ did for us at the Cross. However, after some time, we gravitate towards our man-made laws, or "works" thinking this will bring us victory, and it doesn't. New Believers can get confused or dismayed, and usually no one is there to help them understand.

Some struggle for many years and they end up walking away from Christianity. Others are so frustrated with not being able to gain victory over their sins that they fall deeper and deeper into a life of sin as if challenging God to rescue them. Still others turn up their noses at this teaching, choosing to continue in their own version of Christianity. Once again, the same GRACE that saved you is the same GRACE that keeps you.

Sadly, most of us have learned erroneously that if we try hard enough or do enough of the right things, somehow we can reach a point in our life where we will be as close to God as we need to be. We try to achieve a state of being where there are no more blatant sins in our life. Somehow we equate this "achievement" with "success" as a Christian. Or, we think that somehow on this side of heaven, we can reach a state which is sometimes called "sinless perfection". The Bible does not teach this. Trust me, as long as you are in your flesh, in your human body, you will sin to one degree or another. Our flesh is constantly pulling us in the wrong direction.

For I know that in me (that is, in my flesh) nothing good dwells, for to will is present with me, but how to perform what is good I do not find. For the good that I will to do, I do not do, but the evil I will not to do, that I practice.
Romans 7:18,19

One of the most prevailing sins people ignore in their lives is the sin of pride. Pride is a most deceitful sin. Hence, it deceives the host and acts like a parasite sucking the spiritual life out of a person.

Pride can be compared to small sucker fish attached to giant sharks. We go about our daily business nonchalantly ignoring sinful habits like pride or "white lies" that have become a part of us. People rarely, if ever, see their own pride. Pride is just like those little sucker fish stuck to a big shark. The sucker fish can be seen by others long before the shark knows they are there! If you think you have reached a state of sinless perfection, ask those closest to you if you display the sin of pride. My guess is, if they will be honest, they will say *yes*.

Pride is at the core of most good works done by Believers **who are in their flesh**. If you are working for the Lord, keeping his laws and his commands and doing many wondrous things for God, you may feel like you are good. You may feel like this makes you a good Christian, but if your motives are self-serving, or all about your "feelings", you may be fooling yourself. The Bible teaches us that your good works MAY be viewed by God as wood, hay and stubble.

...But let each one take heed how he builds on it. For no other foundation can anyone lay than that which is laid, which is Jesus Christ. Now if anyone builds on this foundation with gold,

silver, precious stones, wood, hay, straw, each one's work will become clear, for the Day will declare it, because it will be revealed by fire, and the fire will test each one's work, of what sort it is. If anyone's work which he has built on it endures, he will receive a reward. If anyone's work is burned, he will suffer loss, but he himself will be saved, yet so as through fire.

1 Corinthians 3:10-15

The one thing I want you to take notice of in the verse above is the fact that your good works or keeping the law can actually be **burned up** by the Lord. Yet, you will be saved. You do not lose your salvation just because you are still drinking milk! It is your motives, the source of your good works, or your performance that God judges as to whether it is a good fruit or corrupt fruit.

When your good works for the Lord stems from your ongoing, daily, relationship with Him, then your motives are right. When you have a sincere heart to draw close to Him, He will draw close to you. Remember, He is the vine, you are the branch. When you realize that everything you do or can do is because God has equipped you to do it, it is then that you are starting to eat the meat of God's word and have stopped drinking the milk.

God's GRACE means that there will be continual change in every Believer's life.

Remember, every good tree brings forth good fruit! By realizing that it is God's GRACE, and His GRACE alone that keeps me, I open myself up to criticism. Critics say I am diminishing the importance of Christian disciplines such as Bible reading, prayer, fasting, and many others. I am not. Others would conclude that I am creating an "either/or" scenario between Christian disciplines and relying on God's GRACE. I am not.

To compare Christian disciplines *"where we do the work"* to God's GRACE *"where He does the work"* is like comparing apples to oranges. It should not be done. Although they are synonymous to good Christian living, they are mutually exclusive in that our works, or disciplines, are entirely subjective. However, we cannot have any of the Christian life without God's GRACE and what Jesus did for us on the Cross. There is no comparison!

Your Christian disciplines will play a major role in helping you understand God's GRACE and to keep what Jesus did for you on the Cross at the center of your life. When your Christian disciplines spring FROM your trust and faith in Christ, then you have your Christianity in proper working order.

Works and keeping the law demands more and more of you every day. God's GRACE is God supplying your needs in every area of your life. **Law demands, GRACE supplies!** When I am faced with immediate, stressful situations, especially those in which I am likely to respond in my flesh, I instantly realize I am drifting out of God's GRACE. It is then that the Holy Spirit will intercede on my behalf, if I ask. Once again, it all comes back to Jesus who lives to make intercession for us.

...It is Christ who died, and furthermore is also risen, who is even at the right hand of God, who also makes intercession for us.
Romans 8:34

Many will mistakenly think or say that armed with this knowledge a person now can go out and sin as much as he or she want. Nonsense! Nobody puts on a new shirt or new dress just to play in the mud! The Apostle Paul was very clear:

"Should we continue to sin now that GRACE abounds? God forbid!"
Romans 6:1-2

Chapter 12

It Must Be Real!

My people are destroyed for lack of knowledge...
Hosea 4:6

Do you want to learn how to live for God? Take Him at His word!

For me it started out at the Faith Community Church in Tucson, Arizona. The senior Pastor, Bruce Brock, was teaching about Abraham and Sarah being impatient with God while waiting for a son to be conceived. Most of you know the story. Sarah told Abraham to go in to his maid Hagar, and Ishmael was conceived. I spoke of this in an earlier chapter, but what I did not tell you was that I had a "light bulb" moment then and there. Sarah and Abraham devised a plan. Maybe they thought they were doing what God wanted, but it wasn't. They devised a plan in their flesh and carried it out without trusting the Lord. Bam! I knew God was trying to teach me something.

To make it easy, let's look at Matthew Chapter 7:7, where Jesus says, *"Ask, and it shall be given to you; seek, and you shall find; knock, and it shall be opened unto you*:"

These are not magical words in the Bible. They are showing you the heart of God and His desire to stay in communion with us as we commune with Him on a daily or hourly basis. If left to our own devices, we will always take action first: pick up the phone, send the email, confront someone, complain, scream or yell, or whatever it is that the natural inclination of our flesh drives us to do, we will do, in order to change the circumstances we don't like.

This is the exact opposite of how we learn to live for God. We learn to live for God by trusting Him and coming to Him first, not just for the big problems but with the smallest ones in your life.

I could take up volumes of books telling you how many times, and in how many different ways, the Lord has answered my prayers. I could be 15th in line at a lunch counter, and hear one of the kitchen staff say, "That is the last slice of apple pie." I love apple pie! I can simply say to the Lord, "Lord, I really would like that slice of apple pie". More times than not, no matter how many people are in line in front of me, I'll get that pie! Now, of course, I'm making this up, but that is the way the Lord deals with me as I seek him for every aspect of my life. Incidentally, when I don't get the imaginary pie, I thank Jesus anyway, believing by faith, that somebody needed it or wanted it more than I! Things like cash showing up at my house or the electric company or the IRS crediting me when they discover they made a mistake. My life is one of constantly thanking Him for what He does for me every day. After all, when you get to Heaven, what else are you going to say except, THANK YOU!

This is not to say that if you go to work every day you can just sit in your chair, and the Lord will do the work for you. But, He will make your work a lighter burden in direct proportion to how much you ask. You may have a co-worker who you dislike. You can read ten different books, or go to ten different seminars on how to get along with your co-workers, but by asking the Lord to remove the hatred or disdain, He will! If there is any secret to this, it is that you must be willing! If you are at least willing, it is then that God can begin to make the changes in your life that need changing. I'm telling you, if you want to learn to live for God, **you must ask!**

Jesus went on to say in Matthew: *"for everyone that asks receives, and he that seeks finds, and to him that knocks it shall be opened."* The "knocking" here is the asking. I may not want to forgive someone or stop being angry at them, however, if I am at least willing to let God change my heart, then He begins the process of shaping and molding me. He simply waits for me to ask!

There is nothing mystical, magical, or uncertain about the teachings in this book. I think the idea that great claps of thunders and bolts of lightning must strike in our lives in order to motivate us to draw closer to God has been a misconception in modern churches for a long time. Some churches have a veneer of teaching people how to live for God, but have substituted imperfect human substitutes.

Then Nadab and Abihu, the sons of Aaron, each took his censer and put fire in it, put incense on it, and offered profane fire before the Lord, which He had not commanded them.
Leviticus 10:1

When you realize just how much God loves you, so much so that he sent His Son to die for you, your victory over the works of your flesh will come as a natural, godly process done by the Holy Spirit. We may fail, but God never fails. For some, the victory and the knowledge of God's manifested GRACE in their lives may come instantly. For others, they may struggle.

I promise that the times you find yourself "off course" will be the times that you find yourself trying and struggling the hardest. You need to let go and trust God!

When you finally reach a point in your Christian life where you have surrendered your way of doing things, your way of fixing things, your way of caring for yourself, then and only then, can God work miraculously in your life! God will continue to make changes in your life. You will continually learn to live for Him in direct proportion to how much you allow Him in your life. The only "work" you have to do is talk and pray to God. Don't think your prayers have to be long and arduous or poetic. They do not! I know some pastors will disagree, but you can actually pray to the Lord without saying the words out loud. God can read your mind; the devil cannot.

This is what Paul meant when he said, *"pray without ceasing."*
1 Thessalonians 5:17

He was not talking about praying 24 hours a day as some might teach you. But rather, He was teaching us, as I am teaching you, that you can pray anytime about anything, and you should pray about everything. Not too long ago, I told our congregation that I have so many of my prayers answered, small prayers, big prayers, medium prayers. I am constantly and continually talking to the Lord for just hearing me! He literally hears my prayers!

I am nobody special. I shower and shave just like any other man. I put my pants on one leg at a time, just like any other man. As I learn to surrender more of myself to the Lord every day, I also ask Him to take ME out of the equation of my life. I have learned to stop my knee-jerk reactions to everything. I have learned to rest, trust, and to believe in His power. He has never let me down!

God is ready and willing to do the same for you in direct proportion to how much you allow Him to! Don't pass up this opportunity. Whatever it is that is going on in your life, not only can you ask Him, but He anxiously waits for you to communicate with Him constantly and continually. Remember the story I told you back in Chapter 10 about Mary and Joe getting married? Don't be like that with God! God does not want a business arrangement with you. He wants an intimate relationship!

When it begins to sink in just how magnificent God really is, it helps your perspective on His sovereignty in our lives. Nothing can happen to you outside of God's sovereignty! You are sealed! We are all tempted from time to time. We all have our doubts from time to time. Cast those doubts aside and remember who you are in Christ. If you cannot seem to cast your cares aside, guess what? You can ask the Lord to do it for you! We can all take great comfort from the victory that Jesus won on the Cross and realize that it was complete for all time, and it still applies to us today.

Although Satan and his minions can harass, even torture us from time to time, not even the devil can breach the parameters set forth by God. If you are married, in all probability you would do ANYTHING to protect your spouse. Multiply that love and that caring by infinity, and that is how much Jesus cares for you, His bride, His Church. You make up the bride of Christ. You make up the body of Christ. Start acting like it. I don't mean this in an arrogant, boastful way. Understanding by faith that HE is there for you, will motivate you to commune with Him through prayer more and more.

The process by which the Lord implements His GRACE through the power of the Holy Spirit for our lives and spiritual growth is imperceptible. Yet, as sure as you're reading this, the answer in learning to live for God is found on the inside and not anything you can read or do on the outside. This is nothing new. The apostle Paul gave this teaching to us over 2000 years ago. It is the gospel of God's GRACE. It is the gospel that Paul taught. It is the gospel that many have drifted from for far too long. Revival is here!

You may say, but I don't even feel like a Christian. Please understand that your feelings are not the primary issue here. How much you love God or are afraid that you don't love Him enough is not the issue. You need to concentrate your faith on how much God loves you and how much He cares for you, have faith! The Bible says, *"we walk by faith not by sight."*
2 Corinthians 5:7

Our feelings and our moods are subjective. They are constantly going up and down. But, God's love for you never lessens or changes. Remember, it is not how much we love Him. What is important is how much He loves us! Learn to cast your feelings aside in this regard. Go forth asking Jesus to go with you regardless of how you feel!

We love Him, but that He first loved us!
1 John 4:19

Chapter 13

Allow Him

When the Apostle Paul spoke of being married to Christ, as a true bridegroom, He taught us that Christ alone is capable of providing for us not partially, but completely! No one wants his wife or her husband looking elsewhere for his or her needs to be met. Does it surprise you that the Lord works in your life in a similar fashion?

You shall not bow down to them nor serve them. For I, the Lord your God, am a jealous God,...
Exodus 20:5

The arena of Christianity is inundated with people's "experiences". Some of these experiences are biblical and true, others are not. When we learn something new from the

Bible, we should not use someone's "experience" as the measure we place the most trust in. Someone's experience (even our own) should never be the foundation of our daily walk with the Lord. My own experience of seeking God's GRACE in my life and having Him fill me more each day is not in itself compelling evidence that I am telling you the truth. However, those like me who have placed their faith in God's GRACE are drawn into a more intimate and victorious walk with God! We hear His voice and we follow Him! Try it!

If you want to walk closer and talk with the Lord, if you want to learn how to live for God in a more intimate and personal way, simply begin to ask! If you are too busy, ask for more time. If you are too tired, ask for more energy. If you don't understand, ask for understanding. Keep on asking. It is the key to learning to live for God!

The simplicity of God's truest desire to have intimate fellowship with us is being lost through the conflicting messages of the world and the "worldly" church. God has a strong desire to have fellowship with you and to answer your prayers abundantly! Regardless of your circumstances, He is ready and willing to hear from you and He only wants what is best for you. Recently, I was speaking to a good friend who lost his son not too long ago. Unless you have been through such a tragic event, you have no way of knowing the ripping pain and hurt any parent goes through. My advice to him at the time was no different than the advice I have been giving you throughout this book. Ask that the pain be replaced with fond memories of a lost loved one. Ask the Lord to take away the pain. He will! God may answer that prayer quickly, or over time, the important thing is to ask.

Ask for that promotion at work. Ask for restored relationships. Jesus said, "Ask and it shall be given." No request is too big or too small for God. If He knows when a sparrow falls to the ground, He knows your deepest desires and needs.

Over a period of many months of prayer, I continually begged God to empty me of myself. The more I prayed, the more God showed me just how much of ME I was hanging onto; how much I was still insisting on doing things my way. I now have an honest and true desire to have the Lord replace me with Him in every aspect of my life! As He began to answer those prayers, God did begin to replace the old me with the newness of His Spirit. I cannot explain how. I can only tell you it is still happening today! I feel closer to the Lord today than I did yesterday. I finally understand what Jesus meant when he said, *"out of your belly will flow rivers of living water"*. **John 7:38**

I am far from perfect and I know these changes will not end until I get to glory. This is why I am excited to share what I have learned with as many Believers as will listen. My months of prayers to God to "empty me of myself" are in no way meant to confuse you, or suggest that you must pray like I did. Unequivocally, I have been trying to teach you the importance of keeping your faith in God's goodness and to have His GRACE poured out over and through you. Remember, His Grace is poured out and over you constantly and continually. It is all about Him, not about you!

I don't believe we can fully appreciate or overstate the wonderful changes that occur as Believers begin to accept the GRACE of God as described in the Bible. Understanding the foundation of His GRACE and His goodness towards us is foundational to learning to live for God. That goodness began at the Cross of Christ and never ends.

How do you start? You start by believing and placing your faith in God's love and His GRACE: nothing of yourself, nothing of your works, and nothing of your intellect! If you think the Cross was only applicable to your salvation, you will miss out on this great revival of God's Holy Spirit in your life. This quest in your life to constantly and continually ask the Lord to remove you out of the equation and replace it with Him does not end until we get to Heaven!

Nothing in my hands I bring, simply to the Cross I cling.

I am convinced that no mortal man or woman can completely and totally understand God's GRACE and His miraculous gift that He gave to us with His perfect sacrifice. If you think you have a complete understanding of God's GRACE towards you, my guess is you have not even begun to learn.

As I continue to see the results of the changes in my life and the lives of many others, I ask God to apply His GRACE and His goodness in every set of circumstances in my life. Once again, that does not mean I simply sit on the couch and eat potato chips and do nothing! I still have to do what I have to do in life. But, with the new appreciation of God's goodness and His GRACE, you, too, will begin to understand that for the most part, we are just along for the ride.

What an exhilarating ride this can be if we simply learn to trust Him with more of our lives! With all of its twists and turns, the life of GRACE is a continual and never-ending exciting journey. The changes that are taking place in my life and the lives of others are all being done miraculously by faith.

I go to bed thanking Jesus for what He has done in my life. I read the Bible through the lens of God's GRACE towards me now, and I understand that his Word was given to us so that we can live victoriously HERE ON EARTH! Every sentence of the Bible makes perfect sense to me now. Not because I'm that smart. Believe me, I'm not. But, I am in a state of constant gratitude for His goodness, and I shall never fail to thank Him. It is all about Jesus!

I don't care anymore if the dollar crashes or World War III starts, or famine or pestilence comes.

... I know whom I have believed and am persuaded that He is able to keep what I have committed to Him until that Day.
2 Timothy 1:12

With current events the way they are, **"That Day"** may come sooner than any of us think. Come what may, it does not change a thing for true Believers. If you still don't get it, don't panic. Put this book down and decide to try to understand what I am teaching. Turn back to the Lord with all your heart, all of your soul and all of your mind. Trust Him to see you through. HE will!

Taking things to the Lord as our first reaction literally goes against our makeup, especially in those moments when our emotions are running high and our thought process is exclusively focused on with what we are confronted. Many years ago when my daughter, Sarah, was only four or five years old, she was in a playground accident and fractured her skull. I ran to her as fast as I could, only to find my baby girl lying on the cement floor moaning and making terrifying painful sounds. We were in the recreational part of a youth meeting having just seen many teenagers make a profession for Christ. As I reached Sarah, my former rescue worker training kicked in, and I began to assess her condition. Obviously, my emotions got the best of me as I scooped her up for the 15-minute drive to the hospital. As I was lifting my daughter in my arms, I looked at one of the teenagers who I knew was a dedicated Christian. Her name was Holly. All I could say was, "Holly, pray". I was not praying myself nor was I even talking to God. Like a laser, I was focused on getting my daughter to the hospital. Should I have waited for the ambulance? Of course, I should have, but that's a topic for another book.

I was a youth evangelist back in those days, and I did not practice what I am trying to teach you through this entire book which is take it to the Lord! He hears you, and He is more than capable of righting the wrongs and blessing you with His Goodness and His GRACE. He is such a gracious God. To this day, I am thankful that my daughter Sarah has boys of her own (my grandsons) whom she now cares for.

There is no need to beat yourself up over the times that you react in your flesh. It's called being human. Like any skill set, the more you practice, the more quickly you will learn to ask God to intervene in your life. As I said before, the nicest part about learning to live for God is that you can ask Him to help you become more dependent upon Him and less dependent on yourself. We can go to God with anything!

I don't think I can adequately put into words how real and demonstrably good God wants to be towards you. This is not a fad or some esoteric, cosmic energy. This is the true and living God yearning to partner with you and see you through all of your life's struggles. Certainly there are many Christians who will have differing points of view. Some of those may be based on their own experiences. I have done my best to point out to you the biblical truths of God's GRACE, regardless of my own experience. I believe that as we get closer to the Lord's return, the simple message of God's grace and goodness will become diluted or perhaps exchanged for people's experiences.

The arena of Christianity is inundated with people's experiences.

Never lose sight of the fact that you are dependent upon the Lord for the learning, for the growing, and most especially, for the teaching!

I can do all things through Christ who strengthens me.
Philippians 4:13

You want to learn how to live for God? Take Him at His word!

Before I graduated from the Pennsylvania State Police Academy, one of my professors made a profound statement regarding investigations. What he said stuck with me all these years. "Sometimes the simplest explanations are the correct ones," he said. In the scientific community this is known as, *Occam's razor theory*. Exodus 12:22 In other words, sometimes we want to look beyond the obvious to the improbable for explanations of the truth. Sometimes in life, the simplest answers are the correct ones.

As you learn to grow in God's GRACE, and you learn to trust Him more each day, He will miraculously move mountains in your life.

When the Lord begins to teach you the miracles of His GRACE being poured over and through you daily, it is natural to want to share this work of the Holy Spirit in your life with others. Your motives may be pure, but your actions may be suspect. You will begin to notice other Believers who simply do not demonstrate the freedom and liberty in Christ that you have learned. Pray for them, but PLEASE don't think God has called you to change them. God probably has not given you that ministry! **Grace people need to be gracious!**

Spiritual people keep their focus on the foot of the Cross and recognize God's GRACE at work in their lives. This does not allow us time to fret or argue with other Believers who do not believe like we do. It is not important that everybody believe like you do! "Straining at gnats" such as *pre-tribulation, post tribulation, gifts of the Spirit*", rules, regulations are not things GRACE people argue about. You walk in God's GRACE, and let the Lord teach others, unless they ask!

Our dependence on God's GRACE to shape us and mold us from the inside is more than enough for us to handle. Trust God to work miraculously in their lives as well. He did it for you. He WILL do it for others. The body of Christ does not need "splinter picker-outers!"

And why do you look at the speck in your brother's eye, but do not consider the plank in your own eye?
Matthew 7:3

Learn to ask Jesus for the smallest things, the biggest things, and for everything in your life. He longs for you to come to Him daily.

Now we have received, not the spirit of the world, but the Spirit who is from God, that we might know the things that have been freely given to us by God. These things we also speak, not in words which man's wisdom teaches but which the Holy[a] Spirit teaches, comparing spiritual things with spiritual. But the natural man does not receive the things of the Spirit of God, for they are foolishness to him, nor can he know them, because they are spiritually discerned.
1 Corinthians 2:12-14

What is that symbol ن used at the beginning of every chapter?

That is the symbol radical Muslims use to identify Christians. In many villages, ISIS or Islamists will spray paint this symbol on the doors of Christian families so others will know whose heads to cut off. This is my way of standing in solidarity with those Brothers and Sisters in Christ. Molon labe.

Get Pastor Steve's Autobiography!

Written to help the Christian who has been hurt or wounded in a church or Christian organization. This is Pastor Steve's fourth book: **There Will Be No Rescue**.

As a former police officer, bodyguard, Washington D.C. lobbyist, and radio talk show host, Pastor Steve tells the story of his life with a self-help approach he hopes will encourage you, the reader.

From the pinnacle of success to absolute ruin and public scorn, from breaking his neck to coming back and winning a state racquetball championship, from running the most heated Congressional Campaign in